An eye-opening, tender account of how women in the Islamic community have experienced shame and abuse in their suffering instead of acceptance and compassion. Riveting, deeply moving, beautifully eloquent—I could not put this book down. *Covered Glory* brings a message of hope and redemption to Muslim women who long for deliverance, reminding us all of the freedom and dignity found in the relentless love of Christ.

Vaneetha Rendall Risner, author of *The Scars That Have Shaped Me*

Covered Glory provides a clear, compelling explanation of God's honor for the shamed. This book is a treasure chest of ah-ha moments, biblical insights, and inspiring stories. For anyone ministering among Muslim women, Audrey unlocks the cultural forces that so often define life.

Jayson Georges, author of *The 3D Gospel*

Shame is not a burden borne only by women or Muslims. Shame is central to the curse and affects us all. The gospel gives us power over fear and honor to cover shame. Through story, honest testimony, and loving insight, Audrey Frank magnifies Jesus—our shame swallower—and in doing so helps us all to overcome the crippling weight of shame to stand our sacred ground.

Dick Brogden, author of *Live Dead Joy*

Covered Glory by Audrey Frank shows how God transforms shame into honor and creates our soul's poetry.

DiAnn Mills, author of *Fatal Strike*

This moving book is a refreshing description of the gospel and a must-read for anyone working with Muslims.

Roland Muller, author of *Honor and Shame*

Audrey Frank's book is a glorious liberation for the hidden heart. No longer invisible, we are seen; no longer exposed, we are safe. A critical resource for the Western church as we welcome the Muslim world into our neighborhoods.

Jami L. Staples, founder of The Truth Collective

In *Covered Glory*, Audrey Frank does a masterful job of taking us inside the Muslim world and the honor-shame worldview. Through true stories of Muslim women, personal testimony, and solid exposition of Scripture, she uncovers the huge burden of guilt, shame, and fear so many women deal with. She then weaves through this reality the Good News of the gospel to show us the One True God who sees us, knows us, and loves. This is a great book of God's grace that deserves to read by all.

Pastor R. Johns, Jr., The Heights Church

Audrey shares not only from a wealth of experience in Muslim contexts but from a place of deep, personal experience. *Covered Glory* is a welcome contribution to the growing awareness about the topic of honor and shame. Audrey takes a topic that is told in stories a world away and makes it accessible and relatable to the Bible. This book will not only help people seeking to understand their Muslim friends but also those seeking to understand the growing phenomenon of honor and shame in Western cultures.

Dr Brian Hébert, editor of The Diaspora Art and Culture Project

In *Covered Glory*, Audrey Frank masterfully weaves biblical truths with riveting true-life stories to provide understanding, perspective, and practical help that we and our Muslim friends all might live free from the shackles of shame.

Carrie Gaul, Liaison for International Outreach, Revive Our Hearts

Covered Glory will equip readers to overcome the bondage of shame. Audrey shares real stories (including her own!) of women who have experienced restoration by encountering a glory that was once covered to them. Audrey writes with knowledge, wisdom, experience, and authority. I thank God for entrusting her with such an excellent text.

Jairo de Oliveira, author of *Where There Is Now a Church*

Audrey Frank is a storyteller theologian. In *Covered Glory* she leads with vivid stories from her years of work in the Muslim world and from her own childhood. Through these stories Audrey carefully unravels for the reader the inner workings of an honor-shame culture. Not satisfied to simply explain this essential Islamic worldview to Westerners, she also ushers us into an ancient and established paradigm for Redemption. As we begin to see clearly through this new lens we find the dynamic of honor and shame not only in the moving stories of Audrey's neighbors, patients, and friends, but in the Christian scriptures and even in our own lives.

Elizabeth Schenkel, writer and filmmaker at JESUS Film

Audrey Frank transports us into the world of our Muslim sisters. But as she does so, she also uncovers our own struggle with shame here in the West. Her transparency and wisdom shine through as every word points to the love and grace of our heavenly Father. This is a book of reconciliation—between worlds, between perceptions, and especially between God and His precious daughters.

Edie Melson, author of *Soul Care When You're Weary*

"Shame on you" are common words across the Muslim world. *Covered Glory* addresses the issue of shame and honor through a realistic perspective, revealing how the good news of Jesus sets people free. This book is a must-read to all who serve among Muslims.

Fouad Masri, author of *Ambassadors to Muslims*

Audrey Frank tells fascinating stories with vulnerability, love, and wisdom. The stories come from her years of experience living in the Muslim world. Audrey also unpacks numerous passages of Scripture—bringing to the surface the Bible's own honor-shame dynamics, and then applying that wisdom to real-life situations. The reader is personally enriched and well-instructed about ministry among women in the Muslim world. *Covered Glory* is a wonderful contribution to the literature about honor-shame and Christian missions. Any follower of Jesus who is serving and blessing Muslims will benefit greatly.

Werner Mischke, author of *The Global Gospel*

Audrey Frank gives us a personal and practical look at the manifold ways that honor and shame shape the human experience. She intertwines narrative with lucid exposition. *Covered Glory* opens our eyes to discover how intimately acquainted we all are with shame, which steals our sense of worth. All the while, Audrey directs our attention to "the *God of Instead*, He who gives beauty instead of ashes, gladness instead of mourning, and praise instead of despair." For this reason, I am grateful and enthusiastically recommend this book.

Dr. Jackson Wu, author of *Saving God's Face*

Covered Glory

Audrey Frank

HARVEST HOUSE PUBLISHERS
EUGENE, OREGON

Cover design by Studio Gearbox

Cover photo © Alexander Grabchilev / Stocksy

Published with the assistance of David Van Diest from the Van Diest Literary Agency, 34947 SE Brooks Rd., Boring, OR 97009.

All the incidents described in this book are true. Names, circumstances, descriptions, and details have been changed to render individuals unidentifiable.

Covered Glory
Copyright © 2019 by Audrey Frank
Published by Harvest House Publishers
Eugene, Oregon 97408
www.harvesthousepublishers.com

ISBN 978-0-7369-7548-3 (Trade)
ISBN 978-0-7369-7549-0 (eBook)

Library of Congress Cataloging-in-Publication Data

Names: Frank, Audrey, 1971- author.
Title: Covered glory / Audrey Frank.
Description: Eugene : Harvest House Publishers, 2019. | Includes
    bibliographical references and index.
Identifiers: LCCN 2019004512 (print) | LCCN 2019011434 (ebook) | ISBN
    9780736975490 (ebook) | ISBN 9780736975483 (pbk.)
Subjects: LCSH: Missions to Muslims. | Christianity and other
    religions--Islam. | Islam--Relations--Christianity. | Identity
    (Psychology)--Religious aspects--Christianity. | Shame--Religious aspects.
    | Christian converts from Islam. | Women--Religious life.
Classification: LCC BV2625 (ebook) | LCC BV2625 .F73 2019 (print) | DDC
    261.2/7--dc23
LC record available at https://lccn.loc.gov/2019004512

Printed in the United States of America

19 20 21 22 23 24 25 26 27 / VP-SK / 10 9 8 7 6 5 4 3 2 1

This book is dedicated to all who have
been eclipsed by shame,
hidden beneath its smothering darkness.
May you find courage to believe what is really true about you.
You are valued beyond measure,
lovingly formed by a Creator God
who made you to know His love and
thrive in relationship with Him.
You matter. You are seen. You are known.
And you are loved—an insider, forever.
To those whose true stories are told within these pages,
and to the God who rescued them from shame,
I thank you from my heart for showing me the way.

He reached down from on high and took hold of me;
he drew me out of deep waters. He rescued me from my
powerful enemy, from my foes, who were too strong for
me. They confronted me in the day of my disaster, but the
Lord was my support. He brought me out into a spacious
place; he rescued me because he delighted in me.

PSALM 18:16-19

Contents

❦

Foreword

NIK AND RUTH RIPKEN

Names are important. As first-time parents, we sat in our bed with baby-name books spread out across the blanket. Pages were tagged and corners folded marking the places we'd highlighted names that we liked. We investigated the meaning of each name. We tried them out for how they rang together: first name, middle name next to Ripken. We imagined a little boy or girl living his or her life with that name. We looked at how the initials would appear. Just as we settled on a name, we changed our minds. This precious child who would join our family deserved a perfect name.

Overseas, in cultures so different from ours, names are much more important than we had ever imagined. After two fruitful years in Malawi with continuous bouts of malaria, we had to move south among the Xhosa-speaking people. There, in South Africa, a third boy would be added to our family. Our influential Xhosa friends asked for the honor of naming our son in their traditional way. Among their families, when the first child is to be born, the parents of the husband live with the family for approximately two weeks, studying the home and naming the child in accordance with what they witness inside the family. Therefore, children will carry names that mirror what is found inside your home. Children could be named Peace, Joy, or Love. They could also receive more negative names descriptive of meanness, hatred, or infidelity. Our friends, representing Nik's parents, studied our home.

You can imagine that there were tense moments as we tried to be on our best behavior! Our third son now proudly bears the Xhosa name Siyabulela, which means "We are thankful to God." His Xhosa nickname is "Sabu."

Later, living in the Muslim world, a major conversation starter was discovering a person's name and its meaning. Many Muslims place great seriousness on baby naming, believing a name can define and impact the child directly. In many parts of the Muslim world, the child does not receive a name until 40 days after birth at a special ceremony to mark the occasion. The baby's name becomes part of the passed-on, generational genealogy. Many Muslims can recall the entire history of their people, wrapped around the names of their ancestors. Most Somali families can recite 40 generations of names. One man, from a Hindu background in India, could recite 77 generations of names!

Names are important.

Our interactions with Muslim women have revealed to us the depth of shame carried simply due to female gender. A specific name can intensify the burden of guilt one must endure just by being born female. In public, most women in Central Asia will only hear their names spoken out loud by female friends. Her husband will never speak her name in public, and his brothers will never know her name, nor see her face uncovered. When terrible shame is experienced by an extended family due to the actions of a young woman, resulting in an honor killing, her name will never be spoken again. She is taught to honor, respect, and obey without question the male members of her family. She is never to do anything that would dishonor her male family members. Her brothers learn to shadow her every movement to assure that dishonor will not enter the family through this female. The honor of the group, the family, is more important than any one part. Especially if that part is female.

Culture applies labels decreasing a woman's worth, causing her to struggle with who she is, almost from birth. Life forces on women a heaviness, a burden that weighs them down. Ruth has witnessed that it matters little where women live, nor the education they attain; the shame and guilt of abusive names pull women down into a pit that is hard to escape. Ruth observes, "No matter how we hide the pain, guilt, and shame, the 'sin' of being born female is an everyday stain on our self-image." Such a corrupted view of woman's nature follows her into eternity. Paradise itself is off-limits to most Muslim women.

Then the Savior arrives in those cultures, through women witnessing to women. It is when their stories intersect with the gospel of Jesus that the sin and societal burdens holding them captive are transformed and released. Author Audrey Frank has done a masterful job of illustrating the realities of how women (and men!) are held hostage by names given us by circumstances, society, cultures, and families. She bravely weaves her own story into this book to show us how Jesus can bring wholeness, cleansing, and a new life. The arrival of *Covered Glory* is timely, as the church seeks to make Christ known especially among Muslim women who have never known hope beyond the diminished life they are currently experiencing.

Western women often struggle for their civil rights, such as the right to equal pay and equality in the job arena. Can Western women, whose struggle is for civil rights, fully understand what it is to not have the right to be fully human just because one was born female? Globally, it is nigh impossible for women to have the right to be human, equal to a man. Through what avenues can they express their desire to be human, full partners in their homes, extended families, and in the public arena? Jesus makes Himself and His salvation equally accessible to women both inside their homes and inside the marketplace of life. He truly "sees" the woman at the well and cares enough to ask, "Woman, where is your husband?" (John 4). He allows Himself to be touched and recognizes in public the value of a forgotten woman with her issue of blood by asking, "Who touched me?" (Matthew 9). He rescues and then asks the adulterous woman, "Woman, where are your accusers?" (John 8). He asks us, "What is holding you captive?" Jesus recognizes that women matter. He notices them. Loves them. Died for them. He is the God of both Adam and Eve!

Audrey reminds us of how, in the words of the psalmist, God knows our names. Before we were born from the womb of a woman, He knew us. Should we assume that Western culture is inherently good and all others inherently bad? Is it simply a benefit of one's Western passport or the location of our birth that we can receive the message of Christ?

Cultures and worldviews clash. Jesus finds ways to impact all cultures as He blends our stories with His. He sends us to listen, to listen to women's stories from all cultural backgrounds. As spiritual midwives we can help blend their stories, however corrupted from creation's intent, into encounters with Christ. God is sending countless Muslim women dreams and visions that cause them to wonder and ask if there is hope in this world or eternity. A huge challenge faces women who have found love, acceptance, and worth through Jesus. He has healed us and made us whole. Are we keeping Jesus to our Western selves? How and where can these women intersect with us and His story?

Audrey bravely places her life and her story where she can continue to rub against women of the world: the hurting, the outcast, the burdened, and the captive. Within these pages, Audrey illustrates faithfulness in obeying Jesus' command to cross the street and the oceans to share God's grace. Nothing less will bring healing, bind up the broken, and give hope to the hopeless. As you read her book you will find amazing stories that will confront your culture and worldview. Audrey beautifully weaves God's story with the stories of those with whom she has lived, served, and loved. She continues to bring hope to cultures where shame is written across the lives of women like a giant Scarlet Letter, labeling them unclean and unworthy.

God knows our names. Whose name do you know? For whom do you cry out to God?

Reading *Covered Glory* can make us furious with the realities that women around the globe endure. We can choose to ignore what we read and carry on with our daily routines. We can spend time talking about those horrible realities, never confronting the ways that we, ourselves, are held captive. We can promise to pray for "those people, those women." But *Covered Glory* all but demands a response. We must embrace, with action, that which we have read. We are commanded by Jesus to help women (and men) around us and around the globe. The shame related to one's name can be changed by a Father God who is seeking us, calling each by name. God takes the shame, hurts, and pains which this world inflicts on us and uses every experience to help us identify with others. He will not waste any part of our story but will use it to change lives.

Many women around the world know what it is like to experience crucifixion. The psalmist writes that "tears last for a night, but joy comes with the morning" (Psalm 30:1-12). It is time for the resurrection.

Nik and Ruth Ripken
March 28, 2019

Nik is the author of *The Insanity of God*. He and Ruth are leading experts on the persecuted church in Muslim contexts, having served cross-culturally for more than 25 years and conducted research on the persecuted church and Muslim Background Believers in approximately 60 countries.

Glossary of Terms

꧁꧂

abaya: a full-length, robe-like outer garment worn by some Muslim women

'ayin: spring, well of water; colloquially, it can mean one's family of origin in some dialects

Al-Wadud: one of the ninety-nine names of God in Islam, meaning the Loving, the Kind One

burqa: the most concealing of all Islamic veils, a one-piece veil that covers the body and the face, sometimes leaving a mesh screen to see through.

bqiti fia: a colloquial Arabic expression of sympathy meaning, "I feel your pain; I understand what you are going through"

daw': light, typically man-made or artificial

ghairat: (Pashto, not Arabic), usually translated as "honor" in English, describing one's position of honor, a code of integrity, dignity, and pride.

Hadith (pl. *ahadith*): traditions relating what was said or done by Muhammad or his companions, authenticated by a chain of oral transmitters

Hajar: the Arabic name for the biblical Hagar, the mother of Ishmael

hajj: annual pilgrimage to Mecca, culminating in the feast of sacrifice

haram: forbidden

hijab: a head covering worn in public by some Muslim women

hijrah: migration, particularly of early Muslims from Mecca to Medina in AD 622

hubb: love and affection

Injil: the Arabic name of the Gospel of Jesus, which Christians call the New Testament

kufi: a brimless, round cap worn by Muslim men

lesso: a vast, sheet-like cloth worn over skirts by women in some parts of Africa

Masihi (fem. *Masihia*; pl. *Masihin*): Christian

melhfa: a voluminous rectangular cloth worn by Muslim women in some parts of the world; part is wrapped around the body forming a dress and part is placed over the head and shoulders.

mut'a: a private and verbal temporary marriage contract for the purpose of pleasure

nawafil: optional prayers believed to confer extra benefit on the person performing them

niqab: a veil worn by some Muslim women that covers the lower face, allowing only the eyes to be visible

nour: light that is natural or created by God, not by humans

qiblah: direction of Muslim prayer (toward Mecca)

Qur'an: the holy book of Islam

sabaya: young women captured in war by the enemy; in recent times this has come to mean young women captured and forced to become sex slaves by Islamic extremists

salah (*salat* in conjoined form): formal prayer

salat-al-maghrib: sunset time of prayer

saum: fasting

scimitar: a short sword with a curved blade

shahada: the Muslim profession of faith

souq: marketplace

tabib (fem. *tabiba*): a doctor

wudd: love, affection demonstrated by action

zakat: alms-giving, charity

Your Story, Her Story

Instead of your shame you will receive a double
portion, and instead of disgrace you will rejoice in your
inheritance. And so you will inherit a double portion
in your land, and everlasting joy will be yours.

ISAIAH 61:7

It has been said that shame is put upon one by another. No one voluntarily takes it up and wears it proudly. Rather, like a heavy wool shroud saturated with the weight of humiliation and fear, it forces its wearer into hiding. The one cloaked in shame loses her voice...for a time. Shame is not unique to least-developed countries, the seemingly forsaken places. It is not merely the plight of women behind veils, young girls trafficked across borders. Shame is lurking in every culture and every land. Perhaps shame lurks in your own story too.

This book seeks to give a voice to the voiceless. In its pages you will observe firsthand the magnificent work of the *God of Instead*, He who gives beauty instead of ashes, gladness instead of mourning, and praise instead of despair. The Savior is moving in the world today, preaching good news to the poor, binding up the brokenhearted, and proclaiming freedom for the captives. He releases those imprisoned by shame, bestowing on them the favor of the Lord (Isaiah 61). This is the hope that beckons all who come to Jesus Christ.

Hope calls us forth from the darkness, singing songs of deliverance with a clear, resonant voice, promising an inheritance of joy. In these pages, may you find your own voice rising with the voices of women around the Muslim world who have been called out of shame and ushered forth into honor and hope, freedom and deliverance. May you discover that both your voice and their voices share the same cry for honor restored. We are much more alike than we realize.

I learned about our similarities firsthand. I could not have imagined as a child that my story was preparing me for the stories of the women in this book. I had no idea I was part of a greater, silent group of women who are loved and pursued by the same Rescuer, Jesus Christ. Now as I lay my pain, my healing, and my joy down alongside the Muslim women in my life, I can see so clearly that my story and theirs are part of the greater story of what God is doing in the world today. My own pain has become deep joy as I have sat across from women around the world, watching the light burst forth in their eyes as they realize for the first time that Jesus values them, honors them, and completes them.

As a young American Christian girl, I just wanted to be good. I listened to my parents and my pastor, and I went to church on Sunday. I loved God and tried very hard to be a good Christian. But in the privacy of my home, things were terribly wrong. Those who should have loved and protected me abused me instead. Shame suffocated me and choked my dreams. God did not seem to be answering my prayers. Why did God not rescue me? My confusion grew as the despair of my heart deepened.

One rainy afternoon when I was 13 years old I decided it must end. Trembling with fear, my eyes tightly shut, I wanted to die. Life had become too unbearable, the shame of abuse too heavy to endure. I could see no other way to freedom than death. With all my might, I cried out to God to take my life. I knew He had the power to do it. And why shouldn't He? My life was of no value.

Suddenly the door to my room opened and my eyes grew wide with alarm. Standing in my doorway was Jesus, His hand outstretched. *I am the only way out of this. Follow Me.* An unexpected, shocking peace filled my heart as I tried to comprehend what I was seeing and hearing. *Yes! Yes, I will follow You!* The answer of my soul rose like a chorus of hope, its crescendo deafening the fear that had gripped me only moments before.

On that day, I began the long journey out of shame. I realized my God knew me. He knew me and cared enough to come to me in the place of my shame and confinement and rescue me. This was the moment the chrysalis of my old life cracked open, freeing me to fly into hope. I believed Jesus's words that afternoon, and I began following Him out of shame and into honor, restoration, and freedom. I am still making that journey.

I thought my experience was unique. I had no idea that in the Muslim world, girls like me were also encountering Jesus in visions and dreams and choosing to believe His life-giving words. I did not realize how much I was like them, trying to be good, following the religious rules of my parents, trying to win God's favor but fearing I never could.

As an adult, my journey with the Savior took me to the other side of the world, where I shared the love of Christ with all who would listen. One night in the inky darkness, a Muslim woman came to my door and quietly knocked. Her little daughter had fallen into the fire and was seriously burned. I brought them into my small front room and by the light of a kerosene lantern began to tend the little girl's wounds. As I gently applied medicine to the burns, I explained that I was doing this in the name of Jesus, the Messiah. I told the young mother that Jesus had been wounded for us, that He had taken our shame and fear away and given us honor and freedom instead. I was really sharing my own story, the story Jesus had written in my life as I had trusted His promises.

With a gasp, the woman exclaimed, "So His name is Jesus! He said you would come one day and tell me His name. *I have been waiting.*" The joy in her eyes lit the dark room even as tears streamed forth, sparkling in the lamplight. I was flooded with confusion. She had been waiting for me? Her incredible story came tumbling out.

As a young girl, she had been quiet and shy. Her family was too poor to send her to school, and she never learned to read. Islam and animism blended together into Folk Islam, coloring her secluded life with fear and superstition.[1] As a young man her father had accepted the teachings of a Muslim missionary who came through the village. He repeated the *shahada*, or Muslim profession of faith, and donned the traditional brimless cap and tunic. Nonetheless, he continued to rely upon the beliefs of his ancestors, seeking power over the spirit world through appeasement. His children always wore charms to ward off sickness, and when the crops failed, he visited the local witch doctor to discover what he must do to make the spirits happy so they would bless his crops with rain and harvest.

His oldest daughter's days consisted of caring for her younger siblings and doing chores on her family's little plot of land. One day, as she hand-plowed the garden, her father came to her and announced she would soon be married. The man who was to be her husband was more than 30 years her senior, and her father was in debt to him. Her betrothed was a powerful witch doctor, famous for his strong and effective curses. Her father had sought his help for retribution against neighbors who had stubbornly encroached on the boundaries of his fields. The curse had apparently worked, and the neighbor's oldest son had died. Now she would be the payment that would settle her father's debt. She was 14 years old.

One night shortly after her marriage, the girl-bride had a dream. Her eyes danced as she explained to me, "A man dressed in light came to me and said, 'I am the Way, the Truth, and the Life. Follow Me.'[2] He showed me the wounds on His hands and feet, but they were healed. He told me that He is God and promised to rescue me. He said one day someone would come and tell me His name. I have been patiently waiting for you. Now I know His name! *Jesus! Jesus!*"

I sat in silent astonishment. I had gone to seminary, studied Islam and its holy book, the Qur'an, and learned the local language. I had tried my best to adapt to the culture so the gospel would be welcome. But no training could have prepared me for the shock I was feeling in that moment as I realized the exquisite resemblance between this Muslim woman's story and my own. And to think that God allowed *me* to be the one to tell her His name, when He could have chosen any other means to do so! Her story and mine were eternally, inextricably bound together in His bigger story. We had no doubt as we sat there in silent communion that we were known and loved by the Messiah.

A quiet voice said to my heart, *She knows what the pit looks like. She lived there too. And I came to rescue her like I rescued you. She mattered that much to Me.* As a young girl, I was exploited by sinful people, and shame became my master. On that dark night in the flickering light of a kerosene lantern, a woman sat beside me who had also been bound by shame from girlhood. Her childhood cut short, she had become enslaved to another person's sin. And Jesus came to her and promised her hope like He had to me. As I listened to her story, I was ushered into a sisterhood of common experience, common suffering, and common need for a Savior. Jesus had rescued us both from shame.

Perhaps you do not identify with shame. Maybe your story seems far from the experience of the Muslim woman you see on the news, weeping alongside the rubble that was once her home before a bomb blast tore it apart. You want to understand and help, but her world seems beyond your reach.

Do you stand like an explorer on the edge of a great chasm, wondering if it is even possible for you to cross the deep divide that appears to exist between you and the veiled woman you see in the grocery store? As she ushers her children down the street in your city, do you wonder inside if she worries about them like you do your own?

Does the Muslim girl next to you on the bus have dreams like yours? Is she an enemy? Can she see that you are afraid of her? Have you ever wondered if she is afraid of you?

What makes her feel honored? For that matter, what is honor in the first place? What is the difference between honor in your culture and honor in the Islamic culture? What does the Bible say about honor and its role in the restoration of women? How can you practically cross the chasm and build a sincere, authentic relationship with her? How can you overcome your feelings of fear and mistrust?

This book seeks to answer these questions and many more as we explore the Islamic worldview of honor and shame and their vital functions in our perceptions of Muslim women. An understanding of the honor and shame worldview will open doors to friendship and respect. Through its lens, you will become a more effective communicator of the gospel of Christ.

There is a Rescuer who knows each person by name, a Savior who sees each one. His name is Jesus, and He is moving and working in cultures around the world today. God has been restoring the honor of people throughout history. Jesus Christ, the Word of God incarnate, stripped shame of its power and secured our honor forever.

Our journey with Christ may be part of someone else's story. The challenges we have faced, the unique struggles and joys, the private triumphs and the cries of our hearts have all prepared us to come alongside Muslim women and live life with them. We have been equipped to share our common need for a Savior and the faithfulness of the One who rescues women from shame.

Nothing, in fact, separates us from our Muslim neighbors except for our experience of the redeeming power of Jesus Christ. We are not as different as we may think from the women we see behind the veil at the department store, at the soccer field, or on college campuses. Our needs and theirs are the same. Our solution and theirs are the same. The first step toward compassion, toward true comfort, is the realization of how much we are alike.

We serve a God who sees us. He sees every woman. He is the God who saw me, and the God who saw my Muslim friend. He came *Himself* to rescue each of us from shame, because we matter that much to Him.

Our desperation, our life's challenges, our dreams, and our hopes are exquisitely similar to those of Muslim women around the world. And our need for a Savior to rescue us from shame is identical. What is *not* identical, however, is how you both view the world. An understanding of her worldview will aid you greatly in sharing the love of the Messiah with her.

In the pages of this book, you will begin to learn exactly how to do that. You will hear stories of Muslim women from far and near, chronicles of their exceptional journeys from shame to honor. You will learn more about the predominant Islamic worldview of honor and shame and how it specifically impacts women. You will acquire tools to help you explain to your Muslim friend the way out of shame by using examples of honor from Scripture. Most of all, as your stories intertwine, you will be disarmed by the overwhelming love Jesus has for both of you.

FOR FURTHER STUDY

This book seeks to ignite the shame conversation by allowing readers to peer into gripping, true accounts of brave women across the globe who have taken the daunting journey from shame to honor in Christ. Some women in these pages are still on the journey. Others have fully embraced the honor Jesus gives and become His followers.

Where are you in the journey from shame to honor? The study questions at the end of each chapter are an opportunity for you to deepen your understanding of what the Bible has to say about shame as you examine your own position before God. For all who are hiding, may you hear His voice calling you by name, inviting you to become an insider, forever.

Part One

Honor Understood

1

Identity Theft

All day long I feel humiliated and am
overwhelmed with shame.

PSALM 44:15 NET

SHAME: A FEELING

On a small, rural American community, a teenage girl quietly climbed through her bedroom window and leaped to the ground, running to the designated meeting spot. Hidden around a curve in the narrow road, the getaway car waited, its lights turned off in the darkness. A shadowy figure stood by the open trunk. The girl scrambled inside, her small bag landing with a thump over her shoulder. The door slammed shut and she lay in the blackness, trembling as the engine started and the car began its descent down the steep mountain. In this place where no light shone, a second life was hidden. The young runaway carried a tiny baby in her womb, unseen, unplanned, and unwanted.

A suffocating, heavy-as-lead, immobilizing feeling accompanied the inky darkness on that unforgettable night as the 16-year-old escaped in the trunk of a car. It was the feeling of shame, and it would not only guide this mother-to-be's choices but would define her baby's life. This powerful feeling would cause deep agony, painful rejection, and even attempted suicide. But, in the glorious end, it would eventually lead its bearers to find God.

SHAME: A POSITION

One burning-hot day many years later on the other side of the world, a young Muslim woman groaned with the pains of labor. She crouched in the door of her rough-hewn stone house, a silent scream welling up in her chest. The baby would not wait for the midwife. Her nine-year-old sister frantically gathered linens, eyes wide with alarm as she shouted for help. In a distant field, an old woman heard the screams, dropped her wood bundle, and ran toward the house to help.

A newborn's cry pierced the bright afternoon sky as the exhausted mother collapsed on the floor. Then suddenly the room fell silent as everyone stared at the infant boy still kicking in his newborn warmth. His face was horribly disfigured, marred by a cleft lip and palate. The villagers acted swiftly, following an unwritten set of rules. The new mother, father, and baby were ushered away under cover of darkness that same night, never to be seen in the village again. Their names were not spoken from that day forward.

That small family lost their position of belonging, or honor, on that fateful day. According to the beliefs of their culture, the birth of a child with a disability brought shame on their family, their village, and their tribe. The little family found themselves in a new social category that would define the rest of their lives. They were in a position of shame. This undesirable status would plunge them into poverty, addiction, and prostitution. But in the magnificent end, it would lead them to find the God who delivers from all shame.

SHAME: AN IDENTITY CRISIS

The experience of shame is much more than a devastating emotion or being ostracized by a group. In roughly one-third of the world, the part sometimes referred to as the "Western World," people tend to reduce shame to just one more negative emotion, a feeling they would prefer to avoid. In the other two-thirds of the world, also called the "Majority World," its eradication is pursued with vengeance.

In Western cultures, people often talk about overcoming *feelings* of shame. Shame is undesirable, to be avoided. It is a verdict, decided by uncompassionate people who pass judgment on others, sometimes without even knowing them personally. Twenty years after her infamous affair with Bill Clinton, Monica Lewinsky said, "Shame sticks to you like tar," describing her humiliating experience as being "like [having] every layer of my skin and my identity… ripped off."[1] Shame changed Monica Lewinsky's identity. She who once was considered *good* became a symbol of *bad*.

Though the affair was consensual, Lewinsky bore the greater burden of shame. Enduring intense public scrutiny, Monica Lewinsky became a household name. Bill Clinton, on the other hand, went on to finish his second term as president of the United States and left the White House with strong public approval ratings. Monica was not allowed the privilege of public forgiveness and approval. Instead, she was further ostracized and mocked. At times she considered ending her life.

In the two decades since the famous Starr investigation into the relationship, Monica has been bravely taking one step at a time toward healing and rebuilding her life. Today she is an inspiring champion for others suffering from shame. She has learned that shame does not have to dictate the end of her story.[2] Monica Lewinsky has sadly been forced to work through her shame in front of a world audience. For many Westerners, however, shame is something secret and hidden, dealt with on a very private level, if at all.

In Western culture, shame typically focuses on the individual. People are responsible for themselves. Honor or shame directly affect the person, not necessarily the group. As a result, there are resources for the individual that make shame recovery more possible. Self-help books, counseling, and support groups are available. Lewinsky was ostracized and removed from the political arena where she once had the potential to expand her career and position in that group. However, she has been able to rebuild and repurpose her life despite what happened to her 20 years ago.

In the majority world, where belonging to the group is more important than individual uniqueness, honor and shame are actual positions in society. Those who follow all the rules of such a collectivist community maintain positions of honor, or belonging, in the group. In collectivist cultures, the group's health matters more than that of any independent person. A focus on what is best for the individual is often viewed as strange or greedy to those peering in through an honor-shame worldview.

To remove shame from the group, the one shamed in that society may essentially disappear, never to reemerge. The 14-year-old village girl who obediently marries a man much older than her and bears him a son the following year holds a secure place of honor in her family and community. The 10-year-old boy who fasts during the Islamic holy month of Ramadan brings honor to his family and is deemed a faithful son who will one day grow up to be an honorable man. But those who break the rules, who do something separate or different, bring shame upon themselves, their families, and their communities. The girl who refuses a customary arranged marriage because she loves another is forced to flee from her family for fear of death. The woman who was wearing Western clothing instead of a burqa when she was sexually assaulted on the bus is blamed for the perpetrator's actions and later beaten by her mother for shaming the family.[3]

Honor is lost, and shame is the consequence. Sometimes the shift from honor to shame happens through no fault of one's own, as in the case of the young mother who gave birth to a child with a disability in a culture where deformity is deemed shameful and who was forced to move away from her village. Whether someone's deed is intentional or not, the one who diverts from the prescribed route of honorable behavior is forced into a position of shame.

Shame changes one's very identity. The one who once was *accepted* is now *rejected*. The *insider* is now an *outsider*. Those operating from a Western worldview usually seek to avoid shame at all costs because of the discomfort and destruction it brings to one's self-esteem. Many people from an honor-shame worldview, on the other hand, seek to avoid shame at all costs because it casts one outside of society and brings dishonor to the family, the tribe, and the nation. An encounter with shame, no matter the individual's culture or worldview of origin, impacts what that person believes about him- or herself.

Shame whispers its ancient lie: You are without value. You are rejected. You are dirty. You are bad. Some linguists suggest that our English word *shame* derived from a term meaning to "cover one's self."[4] Shame covers the truth about its bearer. Her value is no longer visible to her. Instead, she is covered in a lie about who she is.

SHAME'S BEGINNING

> God created humankind in his own image, in the image of God he created them, male and female he created them (Genesis 1:27 NET).

> Adam and his wife were both naked, and they felt no shame (Genesis 2:25).

There was a time when man and woman knew exactly who they were. They did not doubt, they were not confused, and they did not engage in comparison. Humanity was not on a quest for affirmation, for it needed none. Man and woman, created in God's image, walked with God and rested, satisfied in the deep assurance of their value. Shame did not exist. Their nakedness symbolized only their complete acceptance by God and each other.

This is the earliest picture of honor, the opposite of shame. Honor is essential to both relationship and belonging. Honor is unquestioned value. Honor is reciprocal. It is given and returned. Honor nurtures a sense of belonging, creating and facilitating deep, meaningful relationships. This is the rich and fulfilling environment into which man and woman were created, invited, and included in the circle of fellowship with God and each other. Honor was God's intention for humankind.

But when the first lie was whispered to the first woman, the honor of humanity was questioned.

> Now the serpent was more crafty than any of the wild animals the LORD God had made. He said to the woman, "Did God really say, 'You must not eat from any tree in the garden?'" (Genesis 3:1).

Man and woman began to scrutinize themselves. God's enemy challenged the very source of humanity's value. The serpent questioned the character of God and cast doubt on His character. "'You will not certainly die,' the serpent said to the woman. 'For God knows that when you eat from it your eyes will be opened, and you will be like God, knowing good and evil'" (Genesis 3:4-5). *You will be like God.* Man and woman were already complete, lacking nothing. Made in His image, they walked beside Him in fellowship and had all they needed for life. This was the essence of their identity. The lie hidden in the temptation was this: *You are not complete. He is actually against you. You are missing out. God cannot be trusted.*

When the man and the woman believed that lie, shame crept into the soul of humanity and began its insidious work of identity theft. Stealing woman's and man's identities, shame demanded they take their eyes off God and begin the long examination of themselves that would stretch through the ages, spreading its insecurity throughout all generations. Shame drew man and woman out of sacred fellowship and identification with God. They experienced the anguish of separation from the source of their identity. They found themselves outsiders in a lonely place. Many of their descendants would turn against God and each other.

Shame is a feeling of agonizing loneliness, a state of not belonging. Shame ostracizes its bearer and forces him away from relationship. He must rely upon himself. This leads to radical individualism and an impaired ability to form healthy relationships with others or with God. The one covered in shame has forgotten her created identity, the right given to her by the One who lovingly made her and instilled her with value. She has forgotten that she is made in the image of God, priceless and cherished. Shame has stolen her identity.

FOR FURTHER STUDY

1. Psalm 139 is a beautiful example of the intended
   relationship of belonging between God and people.
   Verse 1 reads, "You have searched me, LORD, and you know
   me." The Hebrew word here for "know" is *yada'*, and one
   primary element of its rich meaning is to understand.
   A crucial element of any trusting relationship is
   understanding. God demonstrates our belonging to Him,
   and His belonging to us, through this intimate term in
   the very first verse of Psalm 139. He understands you and
   me better than we understand ourselves. Read the psalm
   and underline each word or phrase that illustrates God's
   intimate knowledge of us.

2. Reading this psalm may be new or painful for some.
   Perhaps you have never felt known by God, or you may
   have been hurt by those who claimed to understand you
   and now you do not trust God or people. Read the psalm
   once more and ask God to show you today that He indeed
   knows you and loves you. Find a follower of Christ you
   can trust and ask her or him to pray with you for increased
   hope and healing.

2

The Cart Puller's Son

As it is written: "See, I lay in Zion a stone that causes
people to stumble and a rock that makes them fall, and
the one who believes in him will never be put to shame."

ROMANS 9:33

he American baby once hidden in the darkness of a runaway's womb grew into a teenager. Surrounded by lies, she came to believe she was inherently bad. The girl did not recognize this chief signature of shame: the belief that *I am bad*. She believed it was the truth about herself.

One day, in desperation, she sought to end her life. She had been extremely careful in her planning, ensuring that no one would be home that afternoon. As she lay on the bathroom floor, fiercely gripping the bottle of drugs that she believed held the key to escape, she heard a voice calling her name. *Who could it possibly be?* The door opened, and the face of the local pastor peered anxiously inside. "I knew I was supposed to come by your house today! When I saw the front door ajar, I sensed something was wrong and came inside," he exclaimed.

Front door ajar? She felt sure she had locked it. With strong arms her rescuer scooped the girl up and led her to safety, to *life*. The minister and his wife showed the girl empathy and compassion. They loved her exactly as they found her. She never had to perform for them.

But deep in her heart, empathy and compassion were not enough. They could not close the jagged wound in her identity. "Where were

You, God?" her soul cried in the dark to a heaven that seemed silent. "*Where were You* when shame was laid over me like a burial shroud?" A long year of sleepless nights passed as she wrestled with God. Then one humid, summer night, she sat under the stars and listened to a preacher. He was telling the story of a little girl who was unwanted, abused, and discarded. The similarities to her own story were breathtakingly cruel.

With eyes sparking like fireworks he demanded, "Where were You, God, when shame violated this little one of Yours?" The question was the same challenge she had been screaming to God in the most private place of her heart. The young woman bade her heart to be still as she waited for the man of God to continue his mesmerizing story. "Where were You, God?" he shouted once again.

The silence stretched long to make room for the answer. With a booming voice, the preacher described how Jesus answered his question. "'I was here,' cried the Savior. Suspended in agony on the cross, arms outstretched toward the shame-bringers, He declared with ragged breath, 'Father, forgive them.'"

With the preacher's words, the girl who was once a baby hidden in the trunk of a car was concealed no longer. Her hiding place was ripped open, and she sat naked and exposed. The final barrier between her and God hung in the air like a fragile bubble about to burst. She saw Jesus hanging there, saying those irrevocable words. She *heard* Him. And He looked right into her soul.

She finally had her answer. Where was God? He was dying for that shame as it suffocated her and stole her identity. He was giving His life to defeat it, securing her value forever. Now she had a new question to ponder. *What love is this?*

❧

I was the American teenager sitting in the outdoor chapel that night. My question, "Where were You, God?" had been answered, and its shackles clattered to the famine-cracked ground of my heart. Life changed for me. I committed myself to the One who had given Himself to remove my shame. It was the least I could do for such a Savior.

As an adult, my journey of love took me across the sea, to live and serve in a culture completely different from my own. I was a member of a medical team that repaired cleft lips and palates free of charge. My job was to care for patients from beginning to end, remaining by their sides before, during, and after surgery. As a speech-language pathologist, I consulted with surgeons to decide what type of surgery would most benefit feeding and speech in the months following the procedure. I loved watching the transformation from defect to wholeness, shame to honor.

I sought out the shamed and gently showed them their value. One evening my husband and I knelt in prayer together on the cold tile floor of our crumbling house. We had settled in an ancient Arab city where donkeys still carried heavy loads down winding cobbled streets. That night my husband and I prayed for the hidden ones, the children born with facial deformities, concealed in the labyrinth of the city from the prying eyes of those who would cast them out in disgrace. The next morning would mark the first of a ten-day project in the city to do as many surgeries as possible. "Show them to us, Lord. Bring them out of hiding so that we may help them," we prayed.

❧

On the other side of the city, a Muslim woman sat on the soft cushion that served as both couch and bed in the tiny room in which she and her husband and children lived. In her hands, Nida held a crinkled piece of paper, its edges worn and faded. She had carried the flyer in her pocket for several weeks now, pulling it out occasionally to marvel and daydream. In the center was a picture of a little boy, his face wide with a happy smile. It was a grin much like their little son's, whose expression of happiness was grossly disfigured by a gap stretching from the middle of his upper lip through the roof of his mouth. Below, in printed words she could not read, was information. But about what, exactly? The paper had been tacked to a wall outside the clinic and she had stolen it, hoping no one saw her tuck it inside her skirt. She showed it to her husband, and their curiosity grew.

They had been in the bustling city for almost two years. Her husband found work as a cart puller, and she had borne another son. The new baby's lips were smooth as silk, and he nursed effortlessly at her breast. The little one had been deemed worthy of the name of Islam's honored prophet, a name usually given to the firstborn son. His would be a life of honor, unlike their first son, whose birth defect had ushered their family into exile.

The paper she held in her hand must mean something, she thought. She cried out in the only way she knew, using familiar Islamic words of supplication. "God, please help my son. Have mercy on him and on us," she prayed. Her husband was dozing, exhausted from his day's work. The children cried for food and duty dragged her out of her reverie, back into the reality of her hard life.

❧

The next afternoon, as my husband walked home from the market, he took a wrong turn by mistake and found himself in an unfamiliar neighborhood. As he turned to retrace his steps, a woman emerged from the narrow space between two overhanging walls. On her back, tucked snugly into a thick cloth, she carried a small child. He slept soundly, his mouth agape, unaware of the bump-bump of his mother's footsteps over the uneven stones, oblivious to the man who stood in the shadows astonished, staring at the child's bilateral cleft lip and palate.

Surely You are a great God who hears our prayers, my husband declared silently, his heart pounding. Within moments the mother and child reached the busy part of the market district, a place familiar to my husband, who followed a careful and respectful distance behind. As they passed a friend's small shop, he ducked quickly inside and asked for help approaching the mother in a way that would not frighten her. The merchant and other friends were glad to assist and within minutes made the introduction.

Such a delicate conversation could not be had in a public place. The mother did what her family's position of shame dictated: She invited the American man to leave the crowds and follow her to the privacy of her home where her husband waited for his daily afternoon coffee. They could speak about the boy's disability there with her husband present, away from the street gossip.

The sound of children crying punctuated the air as they drew near her street. The secluded neighborhood was infused with the stale smell that settles in the corners of neglected places. Ducking beneath a low arch, the unlikely trio came to a narrow door hanging from hinges lacquered by decades of cheap brown paint. "Excuse me, sir. I'll be right back," the young woman said softly to her guest, avoiding his eyes as she disappeared inside. From within, a harsh male voice mingled with her hushed tones before the door quickly opened again. "Please come in. You are welcome here," she beckoned.

Ushered into the humble home the mother shared with her husband, children, and other outcasts, my husband found himself surrounded by a dozen curious eyes. Word of his mysterious visit had spread quickly. People crowded around in the small courtyard, its broken mosaic walls and crumbling fountain providing a glimpse of former grandeur. It was now inhabited by those who had no other place to go.

My husband decided to explain himself without further delay. Swallowing hard and sending up a quick prayer for favor, he invited the family to bring their son to the hospital for help. The young mother froze for a moment and her eyes welled with tears. Reaching into her pocket, she removed the treasured piece of paper and showed it to him. "I cannot read," the mother quietly murmured. "Can you tell us what this says?"

My husband's hands trembled. The precious paper he held was a flyer advertising the same surgery project he was inviting her to the next morning! He read it slowly to the growing crowd.

Eyes that had stared with curiosity moments before grew wide with amazement and disbelief. The American's visit was no mere coincidence. A miracle had just occurred, and it rendered every witness speechless. Breaking the silence like a thunderbolt of praise, the mother cried, "God sees me and He sees my son!"

❧

Indeed, God does see the shamed. He not only sees them but He pursues them in their hidden places with the singular purpose of rescuing and restoring them. He saw me, the little American girl concealed in a life of disgrace and abuse. He saw my friend Nida, the Muslim mother who, through no fault of her own, bore a child with a disability and consequently lost her position in her family. And in His joyful, mysterious will, God wove our stories together so that we might never doubt His great love for us again.

The unseen are seen by God. The hidden are found. The shamed are rescued, and treasures covered in darkness are brought into the glorious light of His liberating love. Instead of shame, honor is their portion and inheritance. Over the years to come, Nida's son would not only receive surgery to repair his cleft lip and palate, but he and his parents would also receive the good news that there is a Messiah who removes shame.

This chapter has told a tale of two different cultures, two distinct worldviews. Nevertheless, it illuminates one universal experience of shame and restoration through Jesus Christ. The American baby who began life under the cover of shame was rescued and her identity as one valued and honored was restored. The small family whose baby was born with a deformity, who as a result were rejected and disgraced by their village, were rescued in the end, their true identity of value and honor revealed.

The One who died on the cross redeemed every man and woman from shame. That is exactly where He was when their identity was stolen. He was purchasing it back with His own life. This is the power of the Messiah who removes shame and restores honor.

🙙 FOR FURTHER STUDY 🙚

1. Read Hebrews 12:2. We see here that Jesus carried humanity's shame upon the cross and abolished its power forever. But for those bent and broken under shame's crushing weight, this can be hard to believe. Do you believe God has abolished the power of the shame you carry?

2. Read Isaiah 54:17 and answer the following questions.

   - What is the promised heritage of the servants of the Lord in this passage?

   - How can this promise be applied against the weapon of shame?

3. Read Isaiah 61:7-8 and answer the following questions.

   - What do God's people receive instead of shame?

   - How long does this gift last? Underline the "instead" phrases in this passage.

   - What does verse 8 say that God loves? Why is this important?

My Father's Name

I summon you by name and bestow
on you a title of honor.

ISAIAH 45:4

One afternoon over hot spicy tea, my friend Amal and I looked through my wedding album and chatted about our differing traditions. Suddenly she looked up at me and asked bluntly, "Why do you and your husband have the same last name? Do Christians marry their brothers? You and your husband look alike. This is *haram* (forbidden) in our culture."

I was still not used to the misperceptions my Muslim friends often had about me as a Western Christian and, laughing, I shook my head and explained. "Are you kidding? It's *haram* in my culture too! I would never marry my brother, even if I had one, which I don't. For us, when a woman gets married, she traditionally takes her husband's family name. She may choose to keep her own name or combine the two, but typically she takes her husband's last name when they are married."

Her eyes grew big as she scolded me. "Shame on you! You should never give away your father's name. How will you know who you are or where you come from?"

How will you know who you are or where you come from? Amal's question exposed the foundation of honor. Knowing who we are and where we come from is the core of personal identity. This knowledge leads either to honor or to shame, particularly for those from that worldview.

In patriarchal societies like Amal's, honor is traced back through the generations, and the fathers in particular. In Western culture, family-ascribed honor is becoming an antiquated idea, cast aside and nearly forgotten. I envied Amal's confident, secure knowledge of who her father was, who she was as his daughter. I never knew my father and had struggled with shame my whole life. I knew my Father God loved me, and as I learned who He was, I learned more of who I was. But the ache of not having that legacy from an earthly father still bothered me at times. When I thought deeply about Amal's question, I could only conclude that there is a higher source of honor, an ultimate genesis of every person's identity, a transcendent belonging that bonds humanity together and instills it with value. It was for this original honor I began to search.

As I continued to study and explore the subject of honor, I began praying earnestly about writing this book. Over the years, as I came to know and love countless Muslim women, the issue of honor and shame became paramount in my thinking and understanding of their journeys. It was always there, in every story. One evening before a women's training conference, I knelt with a friend and asked God, "If You want me to write about this, please confirm it to me. Make it undeniably clear to me."

The next morning after I finished teaching a session on honor and shame at the conference, a young woman from the Muslim world approached me, tears glistening in her eyes. "I never understood my worldview until you explained it to me today. Have you written a book about this?" I learned she had quietly been following Jesus for almost a year. Her search for honor in the Qur'an had been discouraging and confusing. Faithfully poring over Islam's holy book to prove a case for the honor of women, she had instead discovered a case against it. This bitter disappointment led her to examine women in the Bible and their interactions with God. The honor offered to women by Christ had persuaded her to follow Him and never look back. Now here she stood before me, asking to be taught more.

That conversation haunted me. A woman who had grown up in an honor-shame culture did not understand it herself? Intuitively, she clearly grasped the absence of honor in her life. This intuition, this drive, this God-created need in her compelled her to search for it. But she needed help to understand honor and its implications for her own identity and her own relationship with God.

As I thought about this more and began to engage the subject intentionally with women in my travels, in the states and abroad, I discovered that this young Muslim-background follower of Christ was not alone in her vague understanding of the concept of honor. Many women are aware of its absence, long for its presence, and are confused about what it actually *is*. The question women of all ethnicities and walks of life ask me again and again is, "What is honor, exactly?"

TRUE HONOR

What is honor? Is it a vague and noble idea from the past? Today's world events are forcing us to reconsider this dusty, seldom-used concept. It seems cultures from an honor-shame worldview are encroaching on freedom everywhere with their pursuit of honor. Suicide bombings claim the lives of innocent civilians; so-called honor killings continue to send shock waves across the media. But, we ask, how is killing innocent people honorable? How does such senselessness bring honor? We walk away confused, in anguish, more repelled than enlightened.

Ask ten people what honor is and you will get ten different answers. For some, the word *honor* suggests ideas like honesty, respect, or reliability. For others, honor is the use of certain social niceties like "please" and "thank you." For most Muslims, honor is an actual position in society. It is attached to a group, not an individual. Honor must be protected at all costs or one loses one's standing in the community.

But beneath it all, behind the different cultural and individual interpretations of honor, there must be an origin, an absolute truth. What is the genesis, the standard, from which honor as we now know it has issued?

This quest takes us to God's Word, the Bible, to give us the measuring stick for what true honor is. For God is the author and finisher of our faith (Hebrews 2:2), and He has created and crafted all original thought and truth (Psalm 111:10; John 16:13). Many counterfeits of

His work exist, and they confuse us and leave us angry and depressed. Humanity hungers for the satisfaction of true love, true justice, and true righteousness. When we encounter the toxic pretense of selfishness masquerading as love, corruption posing as justice, and hatred pretending to be righteousness, we are angry. The resulting lack of fulfillment becomes a catalyst for discouragement and depression. Hearts originally created to be nourished by God's truth are instead starved and deprived, leading to dysfunctional individuals, families, and communities. This is surely the case as we consider the many conflicting concepts of honor today. To understand the counterfeits we see, we must study the original.

> I summon you *by name* and bestow on you a *title of honor*, though you do not acknowledge me (Isaiah 45:4, emphasis added).

In the above verse, the Lord is speaking to Cyrus, whom He had called His "anointed" (verse 1). God knew Cyrus *by name*. He knew exactly who Cyrus was and who he was to become. Cyrus of Isaiah 45:4 was the Medo-Persian king who would one day conquer Babylon (539 BC) and allow the Jewish exiles to return to Jerusalem.[1] The prophet Isaiah predicted this 150 years before Cyrus was born.

As a Mede, Cyrus would not grow up personally knowing the God of Israel. He would instead worship idols.[2] Did he ever suspect that he was set apart by a God who knew him long before he was born? We know that he increased in power and man-given honor, to the point of such might that he successfully attacked and conquered the empire of Babylon alongside his uncle, the Persian king Darius (see Daniel 5). In quiet moments, when that great warrior removed his armor and laid down his sword, did he ever sense he was created for a higher honor, one that would glorify God and aid in the victory of a kingdom not of this world?

I find it fascinating that God chose a man of renowned worldly valor to display His greater glory. As mighty as Cyrus was, he would take on a new name, given by God Himself, and his former honor would be swallowed up in the unsurpassable glory of the Lord. Isaiah refers to Cyrus as God's shepherd (44:28) and the Lord's anointed (45:1). God bestowed on Cyrus a *title of honor*, also translated *surname*.[3]

The honor and legacy of the One giving that surname is described in God's address to Isaiah (45:5-6):

> I am the LORD, and there is no other; apart from me there is no God. I will strengthen you, though you have not acknowledged me, so that from the rising of the sun to the place of its setting people may know there is none besides me. I am the LORD, and there is no other.

The Lord's declaration in verses 5 and 6 was both personal and public. Personal, in that it spoke in quiet tones to Cyrus himself that the Lord was the only true God. Public, in that through Cyrus, the world would know there is no God apart from Jehovah. This is so often how the Lord interacts with us. He knows us by name, personally, intimately. He displays His faithfulness to us so that we may first know for ourselves that we are valued, that He has known us since before we were born, and that He is the only true God. Then He surnames us, making us part of His family, giving us a title of honor so that we may display His honor to the world. The duality of the personal and public declaration of God's honor in this passage is a beautiful picture of how original honor, that which comes from the one true God, addresses worldviews of both individualist and collectivist cultures. God offers unfading honor to both the person and the community through the Savior.

Cyrus pointed toward the Messiah who would one day come to set the captives free. The great Cyrus became the anointed shepherd. He is remembered by the honorable name given him by the Lord.

THE HONOR OF A NAME

Honor is all about a name. For Amal, who viewed the matter through her cultural lenses of honor and shame, the common Western practice of laying aside our father's name for our husband's signified laying aside the most important thing about us: our identity. Because in honor-shame cultures, honor is an actual position in society, and one's name is the most obvious identity marker by which society can assess one's position. Names carry honor or shame. People stand in positions of honor or shame based upon the reputation of their family names.

Jayson Georges, in *Ministering in Honor-Shame Cultures*, tells the story of one Middle Eastern man who, after becoming a follower of Christ, immediately began memorizing the genealogy recorded in Matthew 1:1-18. For this man, who had been shaped by an honor-shame culture, knowing his spiritual lineage was paramount to his new identity.[4]

If we think back, we might remember that our own Western culture once held similar values and consequent practices. Malcolm Gladwell, in his book *Outliers*, devotes an entire chapter to the subject of what he and sociologists call a "culture of honor" in the Appalachian mountains of the United States. The culture of honor, Gladwell purports, still exists today in the United States. In examining historical patterns of criminality centered around defending one's family in that region of the United States, he explains, "The so-called American backcountry states—from the Pennsylvania border south and west through Virginia and West Virginia, Kentucky and Tennessee, North Carolina and South Carolina, and the northern end of Alabama and Georgia—were settled overwhelmingly by immigrants from one of the world's most ferocious cultures of honor."[5]

My own beloved late father-in-law, born in a pocket of the United States still deeply engaged in honor culture practices, regularly bought jewelry for his wife and daughters from a small-town jeweler that had been owned and operated by the same family for more than four generations, spanning over 120 years. My husband and sons continue to do business there today, even though it requires a considerable drive to another town. The value of a family name and the honor it represents remain a guiding principle for many consumers in Western cultures today.

Although the West is largely individualistic, a perspective that places emphasis of the individual above the group, an honorable family name is not completely out of vogue.

Summoned by Name

The first element of original honor is that we are *summoned by name* by the Creator God who made us. No matter where we live, in what culture we grew up, or what our worldview is, the honor God designed always begins at the same place. We are summoned by name and accepted exactly as we are. God knows us by the name we bear right now, whether it is honorable or shameful by human standards. He knows all about us and calls us anyway, for He sees who we can be, not who we might falsely believe ourselves to be. That is true for the Muslim woman who practices magic to try to get her husband to love her, and it is true for the Western woman who is a single parent trying to raise her children alone. Wherever we are, we are fully known. And the One who loves us calls us by name and desires to restore honor to us.

Given a New Name

In Arabic, the word *'ayin* can mean spring or a well of water.[6] In some Arabic-speaking cultures, it is used colloquially to mean the spring or well from which a person comes. In other words, it references his family of origin. A pure and clean well is vital to life and health. This metaphor vividly illustrates the importance of an honorable family name in honor-shame cultures. A Muslim woman's badge of honor is her father's name. It reflects her value, her purity, her worth, and her dependability. Culturally speaking, she does not stand alone; she is backed by the strength and valor of a righteous and honorable father. His behavior within the four walls of her home might not seem honorable to a Westerner peering in, or even to his daughter who suffers abuse at his hand. Despite that, as a man and the leader of the household, he possesses positional honor within the Islamic worldview that transcends his personal behavior.

Not only does our heavenly Father know our names, He bestows upon us a new name, His own family name. He confers on us a title of honor. We are given an honorable identity. He has imputed to us the honor that is His very own. Before we acknowledge Him, He has already begun His pursuit of us, calling us by name, to bestow upon us His own name. We become His, and like my friend Amal, we can wear the name of our father with great pride. By this honorable name we are given a status of honor, value, and strength. We are loved. Our position is secure.

I know Muslim-background women whose fathers were loving and kind. I know others who were deeply harmed by their fathers. For some, the discovery of the Father heart of God in the Bible transformed their wounds and became the signature of their healing journey.

Glorifying God's Name

Third, and perhaps most astonishing of all, He extends the honor of receiving a new name to every person through His Son, Jesus Christ, regardless of our own merit. But this raises the question: Why would God give us an honorable name—His own name—even though we have not acknowledged Him? The answer to this question reveals the deepest purpose of honor. "I will strengthen you, though you have not acknowledged me, so that from the rising of the sun to the place of its setting people may know there is none besides me. I am the LORD, and there is no other" (Isaiah 45:5-6). The purpose of honor is so that the Lord can be known throughout the earth. We carry His name so the world can know He is the Lord and there is no other. We, His name-bearers, reflect His honor to the world.

The concept of honor is an innate part of the Christian's identity, though it is little understood by many in the West today. Genuine, God-given honor brings life and restoration, purpose and identity to its bearer. Honor is the exchange of our shameful identity for an entirely new and clean one, the surname of the God of heaven and earth. We exchange our weakness for the totality of His strength, and we bear His name to an estranged humanity. Honor always lifts its bearer up from a place of denigration to a place of worth.

Amal was right in a way. If we do not know our father's name, how will we know who we are or where we come from? Women across the Muslim world are waiting to know the Father God who calls them by name, offering them honor in place of shame. The honor Amal longed for originates in God, was fulfilled in Jesus Christ, and is intended for every person.

❧ FOR FURTHER STUDY ❧

1. Read Isaiah 61:7 again. In this passage we are promised that God will remove our shame and, in its place, we will receive an honorable inheritance from our heavenly Father. Identify three characteristics of the inheritance we receive as part of God's family.

2. The Qur'an (the Muslim holy book) directs that sons receive an inheritance equivalent to that of two daughters,[7] meaning males receive twice as much as females. Compare the following portion promised to women in the Qur'an with the inheritance the Lord promises to all His followers, including women, in Isaiah 61:7.

   > Allah charges you in regard with your children: a son's share is equal to the share of two daughters; if the [children] are [only] daughters and two or more, their share is two thirds of the legacy, and if there is only one daughter, her share is half [of the legacy]; and each of the parents inherit one-sixth of the legacy if the deceased had children, and if the deceased had no children and the parents are the only heirs, the mother inherits one-third; if the deceased had brothers, the mother inherits one-sixth; [all this is] after executing the will and settling the debts of the deceased. You do not know which of your parents and children benefit you the most. This is Allah's injunction; surely Allah is All-knowing, All-wise (Surah Nisa' 4:11).

   > Instead of your shame you will receive a double portion, and instead of disgrace you will rejoice in your inheritance. And so you will inherit a double portion in your land, and everlasting joy will be yours (Isaiah 61:7).

3. What does Isaiah 61:7 demonstrate about the value of men

and women to God? Are they equally valuable to Him and equally worthy of inheritance?

4. How could Isaiah 61:7 be used to open a conversation to the gospel around the topic of inheritance with Muslim women?

4

Burn Away the Shame

Now Sarai, Abram's wife, had borne him no children. But
she had an Egyptian slave named Hagar; so she said to
Abram, "The Lord has kept me from having children. Go,
sleep with my slave; perhaps I can build a family through her."
Abram agreed to what Sarai said. So after Abram had been
living in Canaan ten years, Sarai his wife took her Egyptian
slave Hagar and gave her to her husband to be his wife.

GENESIS 16:1-3

COUNTERFEIT HONOR

I met Hamida on a gray afternoon among throngs of people crowding around a chain-link fence. They had journeyed from near and far by car, bus, train, or on foot. Now they waited and hoped to receive life-changing surgeries at our temporary hospital project. Hamida stood regal and unmoving in the midst of this sea of anxiety. The bright orange *melhfa* she wore swirled and enveloped her in the color of sunset, partially concealing her face from view. When she sat across from me two hours later, I understood why. Women from her area did not typically cover their faces with the large rectangular cloth that served as part dress and part head covering, but today Hamida's melhfa served as her hiding place.

The left side of Hamida's face was completely disfigured by an ugly scar that dripped cruelly down her neck. When I asked her about it, she whispered, "My mother-in-law did it with boiling oil." I pressed her further for the reason. Looking down at her henna-dipped fingernails, she answered, "She said I deserved it. To burn away the shame I brought to her family. I cannot get pregnant." Hamida refused to elaborate further, but quickly added, "I walked many miles so you can help me." I wondered if her family knew she had come. I doubted it. The shame of barrenness she carried could never be burned away with her mother-in-law's horrible act of counterfeit honor.

Hamida had grown up believing that a woman's value was dependent upon having a child. In her culture, having children brought honor to the family, particularly if those children were boys. Because Hamida could not get pregnant, she believed she had no value. When her mother-in-law punished her with boiling oil, seeking to remove the shame Hamida had brought to the family, Hamida believed she deserved it.

We grow up looking around us to learn what is true about us. We listen to what is spoken to us to form an intricate belief system of who we are. Therefore, the belief of countless women about who they are is based on lies. God never intended this counterfeit.

But since the first, tantalizing, beautiful, tempting lie was whispered to the first woman and man, the counterfeit grew to such prominence that entire cultures have based their belief systems, and therefore the treatment of their women, on lies. The truth about female creatures is that they were made in God's image and given equal value to males. But this truth has become obscure in some cultures. Distorted truth makes reality unbearable for many women.

THE BURDEN BEARERS

Corruption always begins with a lie. Honor has been corrupted and distorted, and women are most often its burden bearers. Instead of bearing the identity of one loved by God, cherished and accepted, women like Hamida shrink back into the shadows of shame, hidden and exploited. The truth that they are known and valued by God is concealed by the lie that God is a harsh and distant judge, condemning them to a position of lesser worth than their male counterparts.

Such women bear the burden of accomplishing their own honor and salvation, with no guarantee of success. A Muslim woman can pray five times a day her entire adult life, give alms to the poor, bear strong sons for her husband, fast during Ramadan, and make the *hajj*, or pilgrimage, to the holy city of Mecca, yet still not be sure of God's forgiveness.[1] In the *hadith*, a collection of sayings traditionally attributed to Muhammad, the prophet of Islam said, "I looked at Paradise and found poor people forming the majority of its inhabitants; and I looked at Hell and saw that the majority of its inhabitants were women."[2] Such a deprecating statement by the prophet himself leaves many Muslim women silently despairing, longing for a different existence. God seems a harsh and distant judge, and they often feel far below His notice or approval. Their shoulders stoop lower and lower beneath the burden of corrupted honor.

IDENTIFYING COUNTERFEIT HONOR

Understanding the origin and purpose of true biblical honor gives us a standard by which to recognize and expose counterfeit honor. As we saw in the last chapter, original honor involves three key elements: We are known by name *by God Himself*; we are given value *by God Himself*; and this knowing, this value, is extended to every person regardless of merit. It cannot be earned. It was only accomplished through the sacrifice of God Himself through His own appointed means, God the Redeemer, Jesus Christ.

True honor is antithetical to the idea that rules and right behavior assure acceptance by a higher power. The religion of Islam dictates rules and behavior as a means to God's favor. Follow the rules and gain acceptance. Break the rules and you are rejected. Counterfeit honor demands careful adherence to laws made by man. True honor invites relationship with a God who comes near and whispers our name, bestowing us with unmerited worth simply because He loves us. Counterfeit honor breeds either self-righteous pride or hopeless despair, according to one's performance. True honor fills the heart with relief and wonder, healing our brokenness and setting us truly free. We are accepted. We are loved. We are known. This is the gift of original honor.

Counterfeit honor separates and condemns. It has been suggested by Jayson Georges that counterfeit honor, or "bad honor," occurs when people are given respect for the wrong reasons.[3] They demand it by robbing others of dignity, and it always comes at the expense of other people. Counterfeit honor is temporary, destructive, and contradicts God's purposes.

The Bible describes counterfeit honor as pride or idolatry that inevitably ends in shame. *Pride* is the term used when honor is ascribed to one's self, as in the instance of King Uzziah in 2 Chronicles 26:16: "After Uzziah became powerful, his pride led to his downfall. He was unfaithful to the LORD his God, and entered the temple of the LORD to burn incense on the altar of incense." Uzziah believed himself to be honored, or above, the regulations given to Moses in Exodus 30 that dictated only the anointed priest could enter the temple of the Lord to burn incense at the altar of incense. This self-focused honor led to Uzziah's demise.

Idolatry, another form of imitation honor, is worship given to others. The first and second commandments in Exodus 20:3-4 clearly forbade God's people from worshipping anyone other than the Lord. Yet repeatedly the Israelites worshipped other gods and followed the practices of the surrounding nations, resulting in exile and separation from God's presence (2 Kings 17:6-20). The evidence of false honor is destruction and distance from God. Personal identity, personal worth, rights, safety, health, and life—all are victims of the destruction counterfeit honor produces. This is in direct contrast to the new identity, value, justice, safety, and security true honor brings.

Much of the violence from the Muslim world that we observe in the media is a result of counterfeit honor. This fraudulent imitation goes hidden and unseen by us in the lives of many Muslim women. Like any false promise, it leads to the opposite of its purported hope. Counterfeit honor, ironically, leads directly to shame.

God's Intention

Hamida's shame resulted from this false honor. But it did not start with Hamida. Her mother-in-law and the women before her believed the lie that a woman is only valuable if she can bear a child, particularly a son. They believed that honor could be restored through their own actions, however horrific and inhumane. In their worldview, the weight of honor rested entirely upon them. This is a burden no woman was created to carry.

This belief system is completely counter to the gospel message and God's original intention. The truth is that no one, woman or man, can restore honor to fallen humanity. Such restoration requires the authority and power of a name higher than any other name and the exercise of sovereignty that overrides all earthly authority. This sovereignty is found in Christ, in the name of the God of the universe who bestows His very own honorable name upon His children through His grace.

Counterfeit honor first emerged in the Garden of Eden. God's enemy sought honor and exaltation for himself above the Creator. With enticing words, he persuaded the first man and woman to seek honor for themselves over God. He convinced them to reject God's way and choose their own. They did not know this devastating choice would constrain all of humanity within the bonds of deception. The construction of the false honor idol began with that first fateful bite of mistrust in a loving God. With this ruinous decision came an inheritance of counterfeit honor that has been passed down through every generation of humanity since. As a result, Adam and Eve hid, becoming the first humans to experience shame (see Genesis 3:8).

Counterfeit honor leads to more shame and destruction, resulting in greater distance from God. True honor releases people from shame. It heals and restores the wounded. God's honor draws us nearer to Him. It pursues us and draws us into relationship with God. Authentic honor is imputed by God to those who follow His Son, Jesus. It rebuilds broken hearts and shattered lives. It preserves and protects God's people.

Honor is expressed in diverse and complex ways across world cultures. But honor originates with the author and finisher of our faith, the God who calls us by name and bestows on us His own name, making us part of His family. This is our starting point for understanding exactly what honor is and what it is not.

1. Genuine, God-given honor brings life and restoration, purpose, and identity to its bearer. True honor's purpose is to bring glory to God. Counterfeit honor, on the other hand, is temporary and leads to more shame, more destruction, and greater distance from God. It exploits others for the wrong reasons and is contrary to God's purposes. With this contrast in mind, read the following passages from the book of Esther and consider the questions that follow.

2. Read Esther 1:4-19. The king demanded that Queen Vashti honor him by parading her beauty before him and his men at a drunken banquet. It was against the custom of the Persians for women to appear in public, therefore King Xerxes was actually dishonoring the queen by asking her to do this. In response, she refused.

   • Was the king practicing true honor or counterfeit honor?

   • What was the result?

3. Read Esther 4:11; 5:1-3; 7:3-10. Verse 11 informs us that according to Persian court customs of the time, Esther's approach to the king's presence without a summons was highly dishonorable, punishable by death.

   • Although Esther risked her life to dishonor the king this way, how was she actually demonstrating true honor?

   • What was the result?

5

I Never Knew
I Could Be Clean

The teachers of the law and the Pharisees brought in a
woman caught in adultery. They made her stand before
the group and said to Jesus, "Teacher, this woman was
caught in the act of adultery. In the Law Moses commanded
us to stone such women. Now what do you say?"

JOHN 8:3-5

Babies were snugly tucked into colorful slings on their backs as the women gracefully balanced handwoven baskets with food and cookware atop their heads. They had walked for days to hear the Christian teach from the Bible. Under sprawling acacia trees, they sat and settled on the dusty African ground, leaning in to hear the words of life.

Hours later, as the sun began its quiet descent toward late afternoon, the drums and singing began. With simple words and exquisite harmonies, the worshippers poured out praise to the Messiah. The celebration was rare and priceless.

Afterward, as nightfall settled over the landscape, the fire burned low, its embers glowing a soft orange under the starry sky. Soft rustling and murmurs could be heard as women settled down for sleep on their thin *lessos*, the vast sheet-like cloths they wore over their skirts.

A wizened old lady slowly made her way to the teacher still sitting by the fire. "Thank you." Her words were quiet, barely above a whisper.

The teacher waited. The old lady's face, already lined with years of hard work, labored to form more words. "I always knew I could be forgiven. But I never knew I could be *clean*." Her eyes shone with a new light, the light of revelation and freedom.

❧

Sin has soiled the soul of mankind since the first dirty lie in Eden. It flung its filth on the clean, pure soul of man and woman and stole their sense of value. Man and woman would never again, on their own, be able to make their hearts completely clean. Honor matters because everyone, deep inside, needs to know he or she can be made clean.

Behind the drama of humankind's downfall was One who preserved the value of life. He never forgot. With His own life, God protected the value of the life He had created. He rose that moment and began His longest journey: the quest to restore worth to the human soul, to make hearts *clean again. Clean* is merely a common word for holy. The holy Creator God chased after mankind. His heart was consumed with purpose and longing to make them holy again so that they might be reunited with Him.

The honor God gives is paramount because it promises restored relationship with Him. The universal human desire to have a heart clean, restored, and holy can help us understand the compulsion that drives entire cultures to see the world through the lenses of honor and shame.

Honor goes by many ordinary names: *clean, accepted, loved, good.* And around the world, humankind made in God's image longs to be called by those honorable names. A little girl who feels alone in a prison of abuse, as I once was, longs to be *loved.* The young woman trafficked for her body wonders if she will ever be *clean* again. The man who wrestles with his addiction to pornography wonders if he can ever be the *good* husband and father he wants to be.

The alcoholic fights with all his might to be *clean*, knowing down deep that his problem is more than liquor. The young jihadist straps a bomb to his chest, hoping with all his might that with his sacrifice Allah will finally call him *accepted.* The Muslim woman in the workplace, marching for her rights, cries for *acceptance* and *value*. The desire for honor is a cry for all of these things, and it rises from the depths of the human soul. This is why honor matters.

THE UNIVERSAL EXPERIENCE OF SHAME

We have all been touched by what Werner Mischke calls "the shadow of shame,"[1] regardless of our gender, geography, or ethnicity. Shame is a universal experience. Shame steals our sense of value. It silences our hope. Shame stalks us throughout our lives like a stealthy predator seeking to rob us of joy. Shame was never our intended inheritance. We were created for honor, created to bear the name of the holy God who intentionally infused us with value and purpose. As long as we live in the shadow of shame, we are spiritually and emotionally debilitated, incapable of freely running the path intended for us.

That was certainly true for me, at least in the early years of my life. Born outside of marriage to a teenage runaway, I lived life outside the honor code from the beginning. Honor is a position in society, a place of acceptance within a societal group such as a family, team, or tribe. An illegitimate child who reminded my family of their disgrace, I was born into a position of shame. Reminded regularly that I was different, bad, and unacceptable, I grew up not merely questioning my value but believing I had none. It was in the pages of my childhood Bible, given to me by my great-grandmother when I was seven years old, that I read about honor for the first time. Hidden away in my bedroom, I would pore over the Old and New Testament stories of people for whom God had fought. They were people He had rescued and given new names and new joy. I was smitten with this love story of honor. Over the years it became my own story. Shame was replaced with honor, won for me by a God who fights for the broken.

Years later I met Nida, who intimately understood what it was like to have shame put upon her by circumstances beyond her control. In the years after her family's providential meeting with my husband, her son underwent three different cleft lip and palate surgeries. I celebrated with her as other babies were born, each perfectly formed. Her little family grew, and so did her hunger to know Christ.

Regardless, shame still cast its shadow on Nida's family even as their circumstances improved. The only work her husband could find was to push carts full of heavy loads across the uneven cobbled streets. He began to grow angry and resentful and blamed Nida for their harsh circumstances. It was her fault, he regularly reminded her, that their firstborn son was born deformed. Nida was to blame for their expulsion from the family and the village. Nida was blamed for the family's position of shame.

Her husband's beatings became so violent that one afternoon his blows knocked her front tooth out. She lay on the floor, wishing for a final strike that would take her out of this life. Her beautiful baby girl crawled toward her, crying and seeking the comfort of her breast, while her two small boys cowered fearfully in a corner. Nida's husband stormed out of their small one-room dwelling, slamming the door fiercely behind him.

Several hours later, he returned drunk and boisterous. Allowing the full fury of his rage to blow, he forced Nida out into the dark loneliness of the night, slamming the door behind her. Nida crumpled into a heap in a cobbled alcove, shame whispering to her soul that she had no value.

I passed her on the street one day, not far from my house. I had been searching for her for months. She had disappeared from my life without a trace. But on this bright day, there she was, and our eyes met as we crossed paths on a busy street. We were near my neighborhood, so I invited her to come home with me for tea. She accepted my invitation with one little son tagging behind and another in her arms.

Nida was stripped of pride and had nothing to gain or lose that day. She was raw and real, honest and humble, broken and truly poor in spirit. Devoid of self-pity, she sat before me, an exposed soul. I searched her eyes in vain for the self-dignity and pride I had once seen sparking in her like electricity. I saw nothing in her this day but brokenness, and it alarmed me. I leaned close and asked gently, "What has happened to you, Nida?"

She looked at me resigned, all the fight in her gone, and replied wearily, "I have nothing to hide now. I will tell you everything."

Tears streamed down her face as she explained to me her disappearance from my life. After her husband chased her out of the small room they shared for shelter, she fled to her father's home. He refused to give her refuge, blaming her for not pleasing her husband. She had to find work, and the only work she could find was prostitution. When her husband learned of her employment, he allowed her to see her children again if she would give him her income.

"Now I have no one," she said. "I wait on God." I sat there and grieved with her for a long time, neither of us speaking. It's okay to do that. To be so grieved by your friend's grief that you sit in silence with her for a while. After the silence, as we wiped our tears, I shared with her the story from John 8 of the *Injil* (New Testament) about the woman caught in adultery. Her eyes grew large as I related Jesus's bold challenge to the men to throw the first stone. I watched Nida carefully as a light leapt forth in her eyes. She said to me, "I need you to read the whole story out of the *Injil* itself. I need to memorize this!" Up until that moment I had been telling the story. Nida wanted to hear the official version to make sure it was really true.

I retrieved my *Injil* from the high shelf in our dining room. According to cultural practice, the Word of God was given the highest place in the room, positioned carefully upon an ornately decorated wooden stand. I held the holy book in my hands and read the story of John 8 aloud. As I spoke, the despair in Nida's eyes transformed to hope. Nida saw herself in the story. Ashamed and accused, cast in the dust. Made clean again, forgiven, honored. She ran to Jesus that afternoon and worshipped Him, giving her life to Him fully, while tears of joy dropped down her face like rain. I was disarmed by the simplicity of her acceptance. I expected more of a fight. After all, I had known her for a long time and had been sharing truth with her with no apparent results. But today was different. She had been completely broken since I had seen her last. "I want to follow Him, because He knows me," she declared, right there in my little sunroom, sitting on a hard, wooden chair while the sun streamed over us like joy beams.

Nida did become a follower of Jesus that day, and she took the good news of His salvation back to her community. Today Nida lives outside the city gates, in a crumbling area of town designated for garbage and "unclean" women and children. Nida is sharing her story of honor and shame with her neighbors. She has memorized several books of the Bible. In that place, she has brought God's burden bearer, Jesus Christ, who suffered outside the gates for every man and woman. Her children are growing up to know Jesus from a young age. They will not need someone else to tell them about Him. Their mother did. All because she identified with this woman whom Jesus did not condemn to a life of shame but set free instead.

Nida's story reminds us of another One who went outside the gates, experiencing the shame of expulsion and rejection so that all who know shame might be redeemed.

> The high priest carries the blood of animals into the Most Holy Place as a sin offering, but the bodies are burned outside the camp. And so Jesus also suffered outside the city gate to make the people holy through his own blood. Let us, then, go to him outside the camp, bearing the disgrace he bore (Hebrews 13:11-13).

Our God and Redeemer understands the universal human experience of shame. He not only understands it—He has abolished it. Many women today from every people group harbor the belief that they are dirty, unworthy, and deserving of rejection. Jesus pursues them to the depths of their darkness and shame. No place is beyond the reach of His relentless love. The ground of shame's prison quakes with the thundering of His approach. Freedom and honor are His mission, and all who will be found by Him will be saved.

A PAGEANT OF HONOR

The importance and purpose of honor is perhaps most elaborately illustrated in the Old Testament book of Isaiah, chapter 61. It reads like a magnificent pageant, with the sovereign God Himself walking among a fragmented and suffering humanity, restoring the shamed and bestowing them with approval and favor.

> The Spirit of the Sovereign LORD is on me, because the LORD has anointed me to proclaim good news to the poor. He has sent me to bind up the brokenhearted, to proclaim freedom for the captives and release from darkness for the prisoners, to proclaim the year of the LORD's favor and the day of vengeance of our God, to comfort all who mourn, and provide for those who grieve in Zion—to bestow on them a crown of beauty instead of ashes, the oil of joy instead of mourning, and a garment of praise instead of a spirit of despair. They will be called oaks of righteousness, a planting of the LORD for the display of his splendor... Instead of your shame you will receive a double portion, and instead of disgrace you will rejoice in your inheritance. And so you will inherit a double portion in your land, and everlasting joy will be yours (Isaiah 61:1-3,7).

The Redeemer of Isaiah 61 comes to proclaim the good news of honor. He demonstrates the ministry of honor as He kneels by the brokenhearted, tenderly binding up their wounds. We can hear honor in His cry of freedom to the captives who are lying shackled and chained. He gently leads those hiding in the darkness of disgrace into the light of truth and whispers worth into their souls. He rises with a mighty shout to proclaim the year of the Lord's favor and the day of His vengeance, for with honor comes vengeance. God is the great Avenger, the One who justly punishes those who have harmed His children. Honor exposes injustice and vanquishes the power of shame. Honor returns to the shamed what is rightfully hers. The God of Isaiah 61 is a tender, healing warrior, fighting to restore honor to His broken people. Honor rebuilds, restores, and renews the human soul.

❧ FOR FURTHER STUDY ❧

1. In this chapter we learned that *holy* is another word for clean. Sin has soiled human hearts, and men and women cannot make their souls clean or holy again on their own. God sent His Son, Jesus, to restore relationship between God and humanity. Jesus reinstated genuine honor by taking upon Himself the shame of mankind. With this in mind, read the following passage and reflect on how Jesus accomplished this.

2. Read John 12:12-13. Here we see another pageant of honor as Jesus enters Jerusalem.

   • What are the elements of honor in this scene?

   • How is honor demonstrated and to whom?

3. Expecting the Messiah to be an earthly king, the people cast their garments and palm branches to exalt Christ and usher Him into a human kingdom.

   • How was God's plan different from human expectation?

   • How is the human concept of honor different from God's?

4. Read John 12:14 and answer the following questions:

   • In what posture does Christ put Himself to receive the honor being paid Him?

   • How was this different from the way an earthly king would enter a city?

5. In the culture of Jerusalem both then and now, donkeys are regarded as dirty work animals. The word *donkey* is a word used to insult others. How might Jesus's entrance on a donkey have challenged the view of shame and honor by the people of that time and culture?

6

We Wanted to Matter to God

You know that it was not with perishable things such
as silver or gold that you were redeemed...but with the
precious blood of Christ, a lamb without blemish or defect.

1 PETER 1:18-19

I couldn't understand why the more we talked about Jesus, the more outwardly pious my friend Imani became. When I first met her, she rarely bothered to cover her hair with a headscarf. She wore shirts not long enough to conceal her hips, and she didn't seem to care about her evening prayers. Her mother, on the other hand, adhered to strict rules about attire and was never seen in public without her full *hijab*, allowing only her eyes to peek out. The *hijab*, a head covering worn in public by some Muslim women, seemed to hold no appeal for Imani. As a young college student, Imani did what she wanted to do, following the fashionable trends trickling in from Europe.

Imani was downright excited about Jesus. She wanted to learn everything I could tell her about Him. Peppering me with questions, her eyes sparkled with zeal and curiosity. "No one has ever told me these things before! I did not know how powerful He was!" she would exclaim as we wound our way down the cobbled, narrow streets of the old city.

The more we talked about the Messiah, the more Imani changed, at least on the outside. She suddenly began wearing a headscarf. I had learned that I could determine how religiously conservative a friend was in that particular culture by the way she wore her headscarf. From what I could tell, the tighter the scarf, the more devout the girl. At least, that is how it seemed in public. Imani bought a special headband to wear under her scarf to make sure no unruly hair escaped. The scarf fit as tightly as possible. She was making a public statement of her serious devotion to God.

While we had once met for afternoon walks in the park wearing casual but conservative clothes, now Imani arrived in her full hijab. And we never met during prayer time because the new Imani now prayed faithfully all five prescribed prayer times daily. When we did meet, the discussions about Jesus grew, and we began to read the Bible together.

I was confused. Why was my friend becoming more Muslim the more she learned about Jesus? It took me a long time to realize we were experiencing conflicting beliefs of how one attained honor before God. Honor looked one way in her life, another in mine.

ASCRIBED HONOR AND ACHIEVED HONOR

Social anthropologists suggest there are many "honors" in the world. Across world cultures, honor is understood and expressed in many different ways. However, the two universal ways honor is received or bestowed can be explained as ascribed honor and achieved honor.[1] The two paradigms provide a helpful framework through which we can begin to recognize and understand honor. No matter the varying definitions of honor around the world, humanity approaches honor through these two basic avenues, though at any given time in history, one might be more prominent than another in a culture, particularly in that culture's approach to God.

As a follower of Christ, I believe my value to God comes from outside myself. By declaring me valuable, my Savior Jesus did for me what I could not do for myself. Not only did He confirm that I matter, He redeemed me and sealed my worth with His shed blood on the cross. When I placed my trust in Him, He purged my heart of sin and made me a new creation. His actions, His efforts, and His obedience established my honor before God. I bear His name now and I belong to His family. Nothing can separate me from His love.

As a Muslim, my friend Imani, however, believed that she had to work hard to win the approval of God. Her honor and value to Him had to be earned by her own actions, efforts, and obedience. Worth before God depended on her behavior. The more she heard about Jesus, the more she wanted His acceptance. So she behaved in the only way she knew how to: in accordance with her own set of religious rules, which dictated how to get God's approval. She dressed carefully to demonstrate her chastity and faithfulness. She prayed more. The rules of Islam became her roadmap to honor. For her, value to God had to be earned. For me, it could never be earned by my own actions. Rules had been abolished by Jesus's sacrifice.

We did not know it, but we were exemplifying the two primary human approaches to honor: ascribed honor and achieved honor. Ascribed honor is honor received through no action of one's own. It can come through one's bloodline, family, or birth order. Ascribed honor can also be determined by the amount of wealth, land, or power one's family has.

Achieved honor, on the other hand, can be earned. The United States of America has been built largely on this glittering possibility. Men of no position back in their native countries could come to America and work their way to positions of achieved honor. Such an opportunity was not available to them at home in cultures where one's ascribed honor, or that into which one was born, dictated one's path in life.

When I became a follower of Jesus, I understood that through Christ, honor and worth had been ascribed to me in the eyes of God. Jesus accomplished that, not me. I further understood that I could not accomplish it on my own because I am an imperfect human who falls short of the holiness of God. In my lack, God provided a perfect Savior to stand in my place. When I accepted God's given sacrifice of Jesus Christ for my own shame and sin, I gained a position of belonging in the family of God and a guaranteed place in heaven one day. Not only that, I entered into an intimate relationship with God and began to experience His great love for me. I was ascribed with the honor of belonging to God like a child belongs to his or her father.

As a Muslim, Imani believed that her honor and worth before God depended on her own ability to achieve it by following all the rules of Islam. In order to gain God's approval and live a good and responsible life, Muslims are exhorted to satisfy the five pillars of Islam: shahada (faith), salat (prayer), zakat (charity), saum (fasting), and hajj (pilgrimage to the Islamic holy city of Mecca). Beyond those five global admonitions, Imani's culture has an abundance of religious rules pertaining specifically to women. Outward appearance, such as wearing the *hijab*, is only one of the ways women demonstrate their faithfulness. For even the most devout woman, though, heaven is never guaranteed. After all their efforts to please God, many Muslim women report that they still feel He is distant and does not really know them. They are trapped in the belief that they must achieve honor before God through their own behavior.

THE HUMAN APPROACH TO HONOR

A person's worth in the eyes of her community is determined by a number of different cultural rules. Some people believe that honor starts on the inside, a feeling that grows until it leads to behavior that can be observed by the community on the outside. An example would be Mother Teresa. As a young girl, she was drawn to serve the poor. Her honorable desires led to honorable behavior that has been recognized by the world.

Others, such as some Bantu tribes of Sub-Saharan Africa, see honor as an opinion the community has about a person, which is then projected onto that individual. An example of this would be the head male in a Bantu village. When the crops fail, the villagers expect him to provide goats to appease the spirits and restore harmony. As the eldest leader of the group, he is socially and culturally responsible to be generous because of his position as most the honored (wealthy, oldest, wisest) leader.

It should be mentioned that these examples are but two of the many ways humanity pursues worth, but they merit examination in our discussion of ascribed honor versus achieved honor. The first illustration begins with the individual and is eventually recognized (ascribed) by the community. The other begins with the community and is accomplished (achieved) by the individual. Each of these approaches to honor is incomplete because each begins and ends in human wisdom.

An approach to honor founded on human understanding alone is ultimately flawed. First of all, human wisdom cannot fully comprehend the value of a person. We simply do not understand how important, how treasured, we are to God. If we totally understood our worth to God, we would never seek it from others. We long to know we *matter*.

Although they walked with Him and talked with Him, even Adam and Eve did not realize how much they mattered to God. If they had, surely they never would have so easily discarded their relationship with the one who knew and loved them completely. As a result of that critical choice, they unknowingly sent themselves and all the generations after them on the breakneck pursuit of value apart from God. The problem is, no honor that depends on the opinion or behavior of other people is ever enough. Adam's sons and daughters still hungrily seek approval from a source than cannot fully satisfy. Apart from God, they will never find the fulfillment for which they long. Honor based in human knowledge and opinion can never adequately satisfy.

Like patches of blue sky on an overcast day, we do sometimes get glimpses of the love for which we were created. Those who love and affirm us give us a peek into the deep, immovable worth we have in God's eyes. In return, we honor those we love the best we can, but even then, we do not do it perfectly. If we do not comprehend how dear even our dearest loved one is to God, how can we possibly bestow lasting honor on one another?

Life is at stake in this honor pursuit. We are not just talking about encouragement, respect, and admiration. The honor God gives has eternal significance. And this is the honor we have been given a right to through Jesus. No human being can ever fully comprehend the value of a person to his or her Creator, nor can one fully save the life of another. The psalmist declares in Psalm 49:7-9, "No one can redeem the life of another or give to God a ransom for them—the ransom of a life is costly, no payment is ever enough—so that they should live on forever and not see decay." Thus, the second primary flaw in human honor methods: Value is crucial to redemption. Why redeem something with no value?

Thanks be to God, we are not relegated to worthlessness. He has counted every person precious and unique. Because of His immeasurable love for us, God sent the Redeemer, Jesus Christ, to restore our relationship with Him forever. First Timothy 2:5-6 declares, "There is one God and one intermediary between God and mankind, the man Christ Jesus, who gave himself as a ransom for all people. This has now been witnessed to at the proper time." *This* approach to honor is complete, for it originates in the will of God and finds its fulfillment in the work of Jesus Christ.

We've already established the origin of honor. True honor originates in the One who created every man and woman. God knows each of us by name and has ascribed to every person intrinsic value. Through His Son, Jesus Christ, God made a way for every person to know who he or she is and what his or her value is to God. He bestows upon His children His own name, a title of honor. In response to this beautiful gift, followers of Christ return honor to God in the form of worship and honorable deeds done in His name. The reciprocity of the God-humanity relationship is a cycle of giving and receiving honor, growing in relationship. This is what honor looks like in its complete and perfect form.

The Ascribed Honor of Jesus

Jesus demonstrated both ascribed and achieved honor. His ascribed honor is outlined for us in the first chapter of the gospel of Matthew. This grand list evidencing Jesus's right to be the Savior of humanity begins with the words, "This is the genealogy of Jesus the Messiah the son of David, the son of Abraham" (1:1). Matthew begins with Jesus's position of honor as the Messiah and then lays out His genealogical credentials that made His position honorable. Abraham was the father of the nation of Israel, which, 14 generations later, led to the great king David. Every Jewish person reading Matthew's recorded genealogy would know the Old Testament prophecies foretelling the Messiah who would come from the lineage of Abraham and David (2 Samuel 7:12-13; Psalm 89:35-37).

Jesus's bloodline was impeccable. In an ironic twist, even women considered shamed in the honor-shame worldview of the time featured in Jesus's ancestry. Infamous outsiders in Jesus's lineage include Tamar, who scandalously stood up for her own rights against her father-in-law; Rahab, the risk-taking prostitute of Jericho who hid the Israelite spies sent to survey the city; Ruth, a humble Moabitess with a tenacious work ethic; Bathsheba, the married object of King David's romantic obsession; and Mary, pregnant out of wedlock. *Impeccable* in God's sight, evidently, is measured by faith, not social standing.

I once heard the story of a Muslim man from the United Arab Emirates who read this passage in Matthew. He could not believe his eyes. Right here was evidence of Jesus's right to be the Savior! Tracing back further than any prophet ever had, the lineage of Jesus made an undeniable case for the veracity of His claims. The Muslim man was convinced. He began to follow this Messiah whose genealogical record was inarguable. In the culture of the United Arab Emirates, pedigree is imperative to one's position of honor and validity.

Jesus demonstrates ascribed honor, a position given Him by His Father in heaven. In the culture to which Jesus came, honor and shame permeated the predominant worldview. God, of course, understood this and affirmed His Son's ascribed honor publicly, demonstrating Jesus's position in Luke 3:21-22: "When all the people were being baptized, Jesus was baptized too. And as he was praying, heaven was opened and the Holy Spirit descended on him in bodily form like a dove. And a voice came from heaven: 'You are my Son, whom I love; with you I am well pleased.'" Shame stood in the shadows of the riverbank that day, its accusing voice silenced by the God of heaven and earth. The one born to a virgin, the son of a humble carpenter, had been publicly ascribed the honor of sonship by God Himself. Jesus's identity has not changed; humanity's revelation of who He truly is has just irreversibly shifted.

Luke continues in verse 23, "Now Jesus himself was about thirty years old when he began his ministry. He was the son, *so it was thought*, of Joseph" (emphasis added). This statement of supposition opens Luke's record of Jesus's complete genealogy tracing all the way back to Adam, "the son of God," in verse 38. The Son with whom "I am well pleased" is descended from the first son of God made in God's image (Genesis 1:27). Jesus, the Son of God, would later declare, "I am the Alpha and the Omega, the First and the Last, the Beginning and the End" (Revelation 22:13). Jesus bears the name above all names, and His position of ascribed honor as the Son of God sets Him apart from every other prophet in history.

Muslims believe that *Isa Bin Maryam* (Jesus, the son of Mary) was a mere prophet. He is revered in Islam, alongside Moses and David. The Qur'an says that Jesus is the Christ; that His mother, Mary, was a virgin; that He was a prophet, pure and sinless; and that He would be born, die, and rise from the dead.[2] However, for the majority of Muslims, the claim that Jesus was the Son of God is offensive. Many Muslim scholars teach that the Christian Trinity consists of Mary, the mother; God, the Father; and Jesus, the Son. The implication is that Jesus was the result of a sexual union between God and Mary. When encountering this misconception, Christians can strongly agree with Muslims that this indeed would be blasphemy, never permitted by God.[3] Jesus's ascribed honor as the Son of God could only come through a miraculous conception and virgin birth.

The Achieved Honor of Jesus

Not only did Jesus display ascribed honor, He also illustrated achieved honor. God Himself, in the person of Jesus Christ, entered into humanity's worldview by subjecting Himself to the dictates of human culture and made choices that, in the eyes of heaven and earth, earned (achieved) Him eternal honor. Although God was the Creator and embodiment of ascribed honor, He humbled Himself by becoming man. Philippians 2:6-11 explains to us the extraordinary and astounding attitude of Jesus Christ:

Who, being in very nature God, did not consider equality with God something to be used to his own advantage; rather, he made himself nothing by taking the very nature of a servant, being made in human likeness. And being found in appearance as a man, he humbled himself by becoming obedient to death—even death on a cross! Therefore God exalted him to the highest place and gave him the name that is above every name, that at the name of Jesus every knee should bow, in heaven and on earth and under the earth, and every tongue acknowledge that Jesus Christ is Lord, to the glory of God the Father.

What God is this, who would lay aside His ascribed honor, His pedigree, to labor alongside humanity and earn honor that was already His? This is the God who made you and made me. He is the one who chose to lay aside His glory to heal us, so that we might know true value and honor. We are known by name, by God Himself, and He has given us immeasurable, priceless worth. You and I matter to God.

His mission among humanity is outlined in the beautiful honor litany of Isaiah 61, further illustrating the Savior's interwoven beauty of ascribed and achieved honor:

The Spirit of the Sovereign LORD is on me, because the LORD has anointed me to proclaim good news to the poor [i.e., the Messiah's ascribed honor]. He has sent me to bind up the brokenhearted, to proclaim freedom for the captives and release from darkness for the prisoners, to proclaim the year of the LORD's favor and the day of vengeance of our God, to comfort all who mourn, and provide for those who grieve in Zion—to bestow on them a crown of beauty instead of ashes, the oil of joy instead of mourning, and a garment of praise instead of a spirit of despair [i.e., the Messiah's achieved honor]. They will be called oaks of righteousness, a planting of the LORD for the display of his splendor [i.e., our ascribed honor as a result of the Savior's obedience] (verses 1-3).

Isaiah goes on to describe the result of Jesus's work of honor: the removal of shame and disgrace from you and me.

> Instead of your shame you will receive a double portion,
> and instead of disgrace you will rejoice in your inheritance.
> And so you will inherit a double portion in your land, and
> everlasting joy will be yours (verse 7).

ACHIEVED HONOR AS AN EXPRESSION OF WORSHIP

Once we realize we have been *ascribed* honor through the precious gift of Jesus, honor behavior flows from us as an act of worship. Our inheritance is no longer disgrace. The overflow of this double-portioned reality is everlasting joy. We ironically begin to *achieve* honor here on earth as we imitate our Messiah by loving and serving others. But the beauty and the mystery of the matter is this: Our motivation is no longer human applause and social status. Our desire is to bring honor to the Savior who first honored us. We see here, therefore, that honor is the heart of our relationship with Him. God ascribed honor to us, we return honor to Him, and the cycle continues, all the while growing in our knowledge of and companionship with each other.

Within the human honor paradigm often lies a kernel of selfish desire for public adulation and accolades. But after the human heart has been completely won by the immeasurable love of Christ, secure in its value to Him, no human admiration or award can match the love of Jesus. Our hearts overflow with honorable deeds, giving us a platform to declare the glory of our great Father God whose honorable name we bear.

Honor leads to relationship with God and each other. As we grow in our understanding of how much God loves us, we are compelled to reciprocate that love. What once may have been merely a set of moral rules to live by becomes a living interaction between two beings, God and human, who know and love one another. Grasping God's love for us compels us to see others as also loved and valued by Him. Our perspective changes, and we begin to love others better. We see what we could not see before: We see value in one another, regardless of our outward appearances and behaviors.

Honor leads to worship. When I first began to intentionally study honor and shame, I saw it as a strategy to better understand the ones I loved from an honor-shame worldview and a way to start the gospel conversation more effectively with them. However, as I deeply examined the Bible, searching for honor, I was overcome by the glory and beauty of God. Many times I sat bent over my keyboard, weeping through the writing of these chapters as I stopped to worship the God I was coming to know through the lenses of honor and shame. My original posture as a strategist and missiologist was replaced with arms aloft in worship, in awe of the God who removes our shame, bestowing honor instead. The story of honor and shame became my own. This epic story belongs to every person, and the result of its revelation is an overwhelming desire to worship.

Honor might be the lynchpin of understanding our importance to the One who created us. The position of humanity designated by its Creator is one of perfect love. We are perfectly loved so that we may in turn perfectly love. That position cannot be achieved if we fail to realize we have been given honor by God. We *do* matter.

TWO PATHS, ONE PURSUIT

Imani and I were conceptualizing and therefore approaching our worth to God in two different ways. She was working hard to earn it while striving to achieve it. I had accepted that my value to God had been ascribed to me, earned by Jesus Christ and given to me, regardless of my flaws. While Imani was seeking perfect behavior to gain acceptance by God, I had abandoned my pursuit of perfectionism and fallen upon God's perfect sacrifice in my place. We were demonstrating what the seeking of honor looks like in its two most basic forms. Though we were running along two different paths, we were in pursuit of the same goal. We wanted to matter to God.

My experience with Imani opened my eyes to the longing in all of our hearts, regardless of worldview, to be accepted by God and to our innate tendency to perform in order to gain that acceptance.

Not so long ago, I was like Imani in many ways. I longed for nothing more than to be devout and loved by God. So I set my mind to work at it day and night. Thus began my long journey into perfectionism, performance, and exhaustion. I was one of many in the long parade of weary Christians who march on endlessly through the days, desperate to gain God's approval. How blessed is the relief when collapse finally comes! For it does come to all who strive to earn what Jesus already established for each of us through His death and resurrection. We are loved—and we have been since the beginning. Our value to God has never faded, although our belief in that truth has been assaulted and battered by suffering and shame. Jesus draws near to each of us, no matter our worldview, and invites us to experience honor in its complete and perfect form: relationship with God Himself.

Many Christians today believe in Jesus Christ, yet they trudge the interminable daily trek of trying to earn honor that the Savior has already attained for them. The problem for me was that, although I had placed my belief in Jesus Christ, I continued to also believe many conflicting voices who declared to me my worth—or lack of worth, which led me to work tirelessly to please God. I straddled two approaches uncomfortably: achieved and ascribed honor.

I craved the honor that was noticed and applauded by the world. I labored to be honorable in word and deed. With each accomplishment, I grew further from the quiet, unseen, seldom-awarded honor Christ had achieved for me and the ascribed honor He paid for with His life. For me, the change came when I found human honor to be a cruel and fickle lover. Its appetite was endless. When I did manage to gain respect and admiration, the satisfaction was fleeting. Conversely, when human praise evaded me despite my best performance, I was crushed and determined to try even harder. The push and pull of my honor quest left me bone-weary and disillusioned.

Exhausted by my pursuit of honor, I knew there had to be something steadfast, immoveable, and true that never changed according to my performance. The discovery and acceptance that, as the song goes, "Jesus paid it all," was a relief that transformed my life. As I grew used to this new way of understanding my value to God, the freedom in my life to love others and be myself increased.

The honor humanity offers, no matter its form, cannot set our hearts eternally free. The Savior, Jesus Christ, who has been *ascribed honor* by the Father, has also *achieved honor* for every person through His death and resurrection. This is what honor truly looks like. Those who are willing to peer into its depths will be liberated to love themselves and others across every cultural boundary.

❧ FOR FURTHER STUDY ❧

1. In this chapter we examined both the *ascribed* and *achieved* honor of Jesus. Ascribed honor is honor received through no action of one's own. Achieved honor, on the other hand, can be earned. Why is it important for the Savior of humanity to have both?

2. Paul, the great Christian missionary, had more reason than any to boast about his achieved honor. Read Philippians 3:3-11 and answer the following question:

   • What compelled Paul to exchange his worldly honor, that which he had earned himself, for ascribed honor accomplished and given by Christ? Compare his former, achieved honor with his ascribed honor as described in this passage.

3. Why can't achieved honor, that which a person tries to earn through following religious rules and being "good," gain him or her entrance to heaven?

7

Shame on You

Abraham said to God, "If only Ishmael might live under
your blessing!" Then God said…"And as for Ishmael, I
have heard you: I will surely bless him; I will make him
fruitful and will greatly increase his numbers. He will be
the father of twelve rulers, and I will make him into a
great nation. But my covenant I will establish with Isaac,
whom Sarah will bear to you by this time next year."

GENESIS 17:18-21

Zaynab tells the story of the day she learned the ultimate price she would pay if she ever brought shame upon her family. Zaynab was a good Muslim girl from a loving family. Their community respected her father as a righteous and honorable man. Zaynab's father adored her and frequently gave her presents of jewelry and sweets.

One year Zaynab's family made the long journey to the holy city of Mecca, fulfilling the fifth pillar of Islam, hajj. As they wound their way through the throngs of pilgrims, they heard the sound of angry shouting up ahead. Zaynab's father stretched his neck high to peer into the square and taking Zaynab's hand tightly, pulled her quickly to the edge of the pulsing crowd of onlookers. There in the center was a girl in full hijab, kneeling before several men. One man held a scimitar, a sharp, curved sword, high in the air. In a loud and commanding voice, another announced to the crowd the girl's crime: She had walked home alone with a boy. Her sentence was death by beheading.

Zaynab struggled to turn away from the unbelievable scene and loosen her hand from her father's fierce grip. "Stay here and watch," he commanded her. "Today you will learn a lesson. This could happen to you, too, if you bring shame on our family." Zaynab watched in fear, tears streaming down her face, as the blood flowed onto the street from the dead girl who had shamed her family.

"Honor killings" such as the one Zaynab and her father witnessed have gotten much attention in recent years. We conclude from these gruesome scenes that all Muslims are violent. We all have a worldview, a unique set of perceptions about the world. Through this set of perceptions, we judge the world and live our lives. Our worldview is the framework through which we define and respond to injustice, determine right and wrong, and build families, communities, and nations.

THE BEGINNING OF WORLDVIEW

Sometimes our actions throw us into irreversible consequences. This is where Adam and Eve found themselves. They had never before experienced shame or separation from God. In a wild rush of never-before-felt emotion, we see them frantically trying to cope with what had happened as a result of their sin. Like children who panic after doing something their parents clearly prohibited, they tried to find a way out of trouble. "Then the eyes of both of them were opened, and they realized they were naked; so they sewed fig leaves together and made coverings for themselves" (Genesis 3:7).

Here we witness the first cover-up, the beginning of a phenomenon that would continue for all generations to come. God created Adam and Eve with the ability to know the difference between right and wrong. They knew they had done wrong. They reacted with humankind's first basic emotional response to sin: guilt. Guilt makes us try to cover up wrong and then hunker down, hoping no one will find out: "Then the man and his wife heard the sound of the LORD God as he was walking in the garden in the cool of the day, and they hid from the LORD God among the trees of the garden. But the LORD God called to the man, 'Where are you?'" (Genesis 3:8-9).

The second emotional reaction to sin was shame. Shame forces its bearer into hiding, believing that he or she can never face others again. In the story of Eden, God was on His way to find the man and the woman. They heard His footsteps. But the last thing they wanted at that moment was to face God. Nothing was familiar anymore, and they were not sure what God would do to them. Would the One who lovingly formed them, who walked and talked with them every day, now kill them?

In hiding, we forget the character of God. Shame drowns out the truth that He loves us and wants nothing more than relationship with us. Hearing God's voice calling out to them, Adam and Eve cowered in the shadows and changed the course of humanity. Man and woman have been hiding from God and one another ever since. Shame has penetrated humanity's relationship with God and with one another, and we have become lonely in our pain. In our shame we begin to question if His intentions toward us are for good or evil.

In the shadows of the hiding place, a third emotion wrapped its icy fingers around the hearts of Adam and Eve: "[Adam] answered, 'I heard you in the garden, and I was afraid because I was naked; so I hid'" (Genesis 3:10). Fear entered gleefully, immobilizing them with its evil power, defaming the One who loved them most. Adam and Eve were now afraid of God, the Creator whose fellowship and love they had enjoyed openly and freely.

Guilt, shame, and fear—the basic emotional responses we see demonstrated in the Garden of Eden—have become the primary building blocks of worldview as it emerges in cultures across the world today. Every culture contains elements of all three, but many cultures are characterized by one dominant emotional response at any particular time in history.

Guilt

In Western cultures, innocence or guilt is the yardstick typically used to measure behavior and beliefs. Conduct is judged based on right versus wrong. Westerners talk about things being "right for me" or "not right for me." Social issues are debated on the basis of their perceived rightness or wrongness. Almost every major issue in American and European countries is centered upon deciding whether something is right or wrong or whether someone is innocent or guilty. It is right to recycle. It is wrong to litter. It is right to give. It is wrong to steal. Political candidates are examined based upon whether their beliefs and policies are seen as right or wrong. The justice system of the West is built around the judgments of innocence and guilt, or right and wrong.

This is what Roland Muller calls a predominantly "guilt-based culture."[1] Accordingly, the Western approach to the gospel is also primarily guilt-based, meaning emphasis is placed on one's guilt before God and the need for a Savior. This is not wrong. It is, however, incomplete.

Fear

I once lived in a small East African village. Our village elder was highly respected for the large number of goats and sheep he owned. It took several young boys to herd the animals every day across the rolling hills. One day the elder's aging mother became sick. She was seriously ill, so the people called upon the witch doctor.

Over the course of two weeks, more than half the elder's livestock were slaughtered. After consulting the spirits, the witch doctor had determined the village ancestors were angry with the elder for planting a new kind of bean that year along with the typical corn. Thus, they had brought this sickness upon his mother. To appease their anger, the spirits now demanded the sacrifice of many animals. I am sorry to say that the elderly woman died at the end of those two weeks of long nights, animal sacrifices, and frantic singing to the spirits.

My neighbors in that village were driven by fear, and it dominated their worldview. They practice what is called *animism*, or worship and appeasement of the spirit world. They believe that gods and spirits exist in the universe, and they must live peaceably with those unseen authorities by appeasing them.[2] In such cultures, fear is the primary building block of their worldview.

Power is an important concept in fear-based cultures. Animists believe they are at the mercy of spirits who can be easily offended, bringing punishment down on individuals and whole communities. When something bad happens, the assumption in fear-based cultures is that the spirits have been angered. Spiritual power has been knocked out of balance and must be restored or punishment will result. The fear of punishment can only be relieved by appeasing the offended spirit or calling out to a greater spiritual power. If it is believed that a spirit has been offended, as in the case of the village grandmother, great effort will be made to please the spirits and restore peace to the community.

Shame

Many cultures around the world, especially in the Middle East and Asia, exhibit a predominantly shame-based worldview. The honor-shame worldview features strongly in *collectivist societies*, those that make decisions based on how they impact the group to which one belongs. Within these cultures, honor is an actual position in society. Shame robs one of that position, moving him or her outside the group. Isolation and separation are seen as highly undesirable. Avoiding shame is of utmost importance.

Westerners are often confused by this perspective. Individualist societies emphasize independence and original thoughts and ideas. Decisions that appear to deny the individual his or her uniqueness seem oppressive or unjust through the eyes of the Western worldview. To one with an honor-shame worldview, however, the group is always more important than one's own rights.

A basic understanding of worldview prepares us to examine honor and shame in Islamic cultures more objectively. However, I must qualify this. The more I learn about how my Muslim friends view honor and shame, the more I realize all I have yet to learn. This book is only a glimpse into an intricate and complex way of viewing and making sense of the world. Worldviews are cultivated over centuries. No one book can thoroughly explain all their nuances. Even a small amount of understanding of the honor-shame worldview, however, can produce a tremendous result as we seek to build authentic relationships between cultures. For a more thorough examination of the three worldviews presented in this chapter, see the appendix for recommended resources.

NOT A CULTURE OF VIOLENCE

We were not often out at night in the marketplace of the old Arab city. On this particular evening, a visit with friends had gone later than expected and we found ourselves navigating the twists and turns of the narrow streets with our sleepy children in tow. The air pulsed with sound. The meat seller's rap-shouting declaring his discounted last cuts of meat to the crowds thumped like a bass drum. The silversmiths' tap-tap-tapping as they hammered their fine chisels into soft silver, creating intricate geometrical patterns, danced in the background. Underneath it all was the buzz of a thousand conversations as families like ours took in the cacophony of sights and sounds of the night souq, the busy market that sold everything one could possibly need.

Suddenly and without warning, the masses stopped in their tracks, jamming the passageway. A different feeling immediately filled the thick air: panic and fear. Mothers ran with their babies; fathers scooped up little children and ducked into alcoves. We huddled along the wall to avoid being crushed. Two men were fighting in the middle of the street, the glint of their curved knives flashing in the lamplights. Snatches of angry words reached our ears, words like "shame," "kill," and "God forbid." We had stumbled upon a battle for honor. The bazaar that had only moments before resounded with family laughter now emptied out, replaced by the sounds of an age-old effort to vanquish shame.

No society, in the hearts of its men and women, likes violence. Confrontation, rejection, and death are undesirable in every culture. Civilizations create intricate systems to avoid reaching the point of violence. Violence is a last resort. This is true in Western cultures and this is true in Islamic cultures. If we take pause and lay aside our presuppositions for a moment, we observe several other, nonviolent ways Muslims attempt to deal with shame.

Avoidance

Let's go back to Zaynab and her father for a moment. A Western, innocence-guilt worldview responds to their experience indignantly, deeming her father wrong to have forced Zaynab to witness the beheading of a girl who had done nothing criminal. From a Muslim perspective, what he did demonstrated the first and mildest form of handling shame: *avoiding it altogether.*

By imposing on his daughter the unforgettable scene, he was seeking to avoid the same thing happening in his own family. Through his worldview of honor and shame, he believed he was showing love to his daughter by warning her. He was saving her from the same fate, from a life of shame and possibly even death. Furthermore, he was saving his family from the same fate, that of losing their position in society through shame. Someone with an honor-shame worldview is always thinking about behavior within the context of the group, not the individual. They are constantly thinking about how to avoid shame.

A colleague shared with me a story that illustrates distinctly the desire to avoid shame. Paul's friend, Rashaad, asked him where to invest one hundred thousand dollars he had inherited. Paul worked out a plan with him to open a Western-style butcher shop with steaks, roasts, and other cuts that Westerners and people who had lived in the West were looking for but could not find. Together they worked out how Rashaad's cuts could be transported and sold in stores all across the city. The plan appeared to be pleasing and acceptable to Rashaad, who committed many hours to developing it with Paul. But, in the end, Rashaad chose to buy an olive grove instead. Paul was bewildered.

When asked why, Rashaad said that if the olive crop were to fail, it would be because all the olive groves in the country had failed, and no shame would be attached to his family. But if he invested in the butcher shop and it failed, he alone would bear the shame. Rashaad chose the mildest form of handling shame: avoiding it altogether.

This concept can be confusing and frustrating to Westerners, especially those working with men and women from honor-shame cultures in business or other cooperative endeavors. This story, along with that of Zaynab's father, demonstrates how deeply honor and shame affect men as well as women. They fear failure and the consequent shame it brings. As a friend of mine says, this is why men from Islamic cultures tend not to be adventurers and entrepreneurs. They are consumed with avoiding shame. Perhaps it occupies their minds as much as it does those of women, although they bear it differently.

Covering

An adage in our family goes like this: Hospitality means that you treat friends like family and family like friends. We did not create the expression, but we have often quoted it with a smile. Our house is usually full of family and friends, and our hearts are set on making all of them feel at home and accepted.

One day that attitude backfired, and the results were perplexing and discouraging. I had left my camera on the counter in our kitchen during a gathering of the underground church that met in our home each week. We did not really meet "underground," but the term had come to describe church gatherings that happened in secret during times of persecution or in places where Christian worship was illegal. This particular day we were having a celebration, and the people who filled our home were friends. Furthermore, they were followers of Christ, former Muslims who had made the courageous and sincere decision to disobey their government, leave Islam, and become *Masihin*, or Christians. The only recourse was to gather behind closed doors with other Jesus followers. Today we were rejoicing with a new couple who had recently gotten married.

Slipping into the kitchen to check the teakettle, I put the camera on the counter and promptly forgot about it in the hustle of preparations. Pictures had already been taken, and I didn't need it again right away.

A couple of hours after the guests had left, I remembered the camera and went into the kitchen to retrieve it. It was not on the wooden cabinet where I had left it. Assuming my husband had put it away, I asked him about it. Nope, he had not seen it. My sons were too small at the time to reach the cabinet, so I knew they hadn't played with it. I went down the mental list of possibilities, eliminating each one.

Surely it couldn't have been stolen by one of our guests! I thought to myself incredulously. We were a close, trusted group. My husband and I had always done right by these people, generously giving ourselves, our home, and our time. It would not make sense, would not be right for them to respond to our generosity by stealing from us. I was simmering in my innocence-guilt worldview, trying to make sense of the situation. After lengthy conversations and analysis of the afternoon's events, my husband and I realized it could have been only one person. As reality dawned on us, discouragement and disappointment weighed heavy on our hearts.

The next week the person we suspected appeared in all new trendy clothes and shoes, having evidently been on an uncharacteristic shopping spree. Surely not! we thought. Later that week we received confirmation from another person that the culprit was, indeed, who we thought. *How on earth do we confront this?* we wondered.

We decided to talk to the pastor about it. Many of the church members were also his family members, so we assumed he would understand how to sensitively approach the situation. In our naive understanding of honor and shame cultures, we thought we were preserving the thief's honor by bringing in a mediator from the same family and pursuing a logical solution.

Imagine our shock when the pastor made up a cover story! Instead of confronting the thief for us and seeking reconciliation and justice, he covered the crime and made it clear the conversation would gain no more traction. My husband and I did not understand it at the time, but the pastor was illustrating another stage of handling shame: *covering.* He was a follower of Christ, but that had not converted his worldview to a Western one. Nor should it. Too often, cross-cultural Christians confuse worldview with righteousness. From our Western, right-versus-wrong worldview, sin is to be confronted. From our pastor friend's perspective, shame is to be avoided, and if that is not possible, it must be covered.

I realize now, with the clarity of retrospect, what was at stake for him: loss of position in the small community of believers and loss of a safe location to meet for worship. In his position as an elder leader, he had a cultural responsibility to protect the women in his family. He did this by covering the shame one family member brought by stealing from us. His eyes admitted her crime even as his words covered her shame. If shame cannot be avoided, it will be covered in Islamic societies, if at all possible. We did not have the experience and worldview understanding to see his struggle as noble at the time. I wish we had. His behavior looked like dishonesty to us, and we were incensed.

It took us a long time to work through our confusion and disappointment. That was time we could have spent growing in relationship, discipleship, and worship.

Denial

I was so full I could not even sit upright. Leaning back gratefully on the luxurious couch behind me, I caught my friend Nour's twinkling eyes. "Eat more! More is coming! You can't stop yet!" About that same moment her aunt Atiya walked in, bearing a heavy clay dish piled high with steaming rice and lamb. Placing it deftly in the center of the table, she quickly tucked her head down and left the room as quietly as she had come.

"Thank you, Atiya!" I called after her. She did not respond.

"She isn't here," said Nour.

I was confused. I thought she meant that Atiya had left the house. "Where did she go? Surely not for more food!" I said with a laugh.

"She's in the kitchen, her place," replied Nour nonchalantly.

"Oh. I thought you said she isn't here."

"She's not. It's an expression," explained Nour, not really explaining at all.

I rolled my eyes on the inside. *Not, "it's an expression" again,* I thought to myself. I hated when my friends said that in response to my misunderstandings in Arabic. Just when I thought I was making progress with the language, I would run into an obscure expression that seemed impossible to understand. Nour must have noticed my dismay and was feeling unusually generous that day. "Okay. I'll explain it to you. She isn't married anymore, so she isn't here." This seemed to Nour to be a satisfactory explanation.

I was too mortified to probe for a deeper explanation. I loved Atiya and I was expected to eat her delicious food, but she wasn't allowed to receive my gratitude for it. She wasn't allowed to exist, except to make the food appear and the dirty dishes to disappear. A heaviness settled around my heart and I lost my appetite.

I felt lied to. But after deeper consideration, I perceived that Nour's insistence Atiya was not there, when she actually was, was *not* a lie in my friend's mind. But the reason why she would say that was obscure to me. Later I asked another friend about the expression. She explained to me that when a woman is sent away by her husband, back to her father's home, she brings shame on her father's house. The way that shame is handled is by denying her existence. Such a woman will often accept the arrangement in exchange for her life, room, and board. Nour didn't consider her attitude toward Atiya to be wrong. She did not lie to me, according to her worldview. I don't really think she evaluated it closely. She was merely doing what women in her culture had done for centuries to cope with shame: She was denying its existence.

A Last Resort

We have taken a closer look at three unofficial but clearly observable ways Islamic cultures handle shame. These three strategies can be seen across North Africa and the Middle East, from the arid plains of the Fertile Crescent that stretch from Egypt to Iraq and even in the nomadic sands of the Sahara. In the wake of the greatest refugee crisis in history, they can be witnessed in Western nations today as well. What has received the most modern attention, however, is not these milder methods to restore honor, but rather the last resort, the kind of violence Zaynab and her father witnessed in the beginning of our chapter.

When avoiding, covering, and denying have failed, all that is left is purging. Purging is the last resort in an effort to deal with shame. It might manifest in the form of expulsion from the family or tribe. Purging may be like Hamida's story in chapter 4, whose mother-in-law threw boiling oil on her to supposedly remove the shame her barrenness had brought on the woman's family. Ultimately, purging can take the form of death.

A STRUGGLE AGAINST SIN

The struggle in honor-shame cultures to restore honor is, at its heart, the age-old struggle against sin. Avoiding shame or managing it is a way of life, an effort to cope with sin. But these carefully constructed methods will never work, for they have no power to remove sin from human hearts. This is where the gospel so beautifully responds to the shame battle. Jesus knew we cannot avoid the shame. So He embraced it head-on, endured it, despised it, and ultimately defeated it. This is beautifully illustrated in Hebrews:

> ...fixing our eyes on Jesus, the author and perfecter of faith, who for the joy set before Him endured the cross, despising the shame, and has sat down at the right hand of the throne of God (12:2 NASB).

The human attempt to manage shame through covering or purging is a mutation of the salvific covering and purging of sin and shame done by God Himself. The problem with these impaired human methods is that all have fallen short of the glory of God. We are disqualified deliverers.

> For all have sinned and fall short of the glory of God (Romans 3:23).

We have been sentenced to separation from God, and no one but Jesus Christ can bring us back into relationship with God. Romans 3:23 balances both *sin* and *shame* (falling short of God's glory) as obstacles we all face in life's most crucial dilemma. No amount of covering or seeking to purge my or another's shame will suffice. There must be divine intervention by One completely holy (clean, without shame) and innocent (without guilt). That one is the Messiah, Jesus.

THE GREAT COVERER

Throughout the story of God's great love for humanity, we see Him covering our shame. It began with the first blood ever shed. In Genesis 3:21, animals were slaughtered so shame could be covered and skins made for Adam and Eve to wear. This first blood sacrifice to cover man and woman's shame foreshadowed the blood Jesus would one day shed to cover the shame of humanity forever.[3]

In Ruth 3, we see another powerful example of covering. Ruth had originally married Mahlon, son of Elimelech and Naomi. Mahlon and his family were Israelites from Judah. After the deaths of both her father-in-law and Mahlon, Ruth moved to Bethlehem with her mother-in-law, Naomi. According to Levitical law, if a woman's husband died and she was left childless, her husband's closest male relative was required to marry her so an heir could be born to carry on the name of the dead man. This relative was known as a "kinsman redeemer."[4] Upon her mother-in-law's instruction, Ruth approached her kinsman redeemer, Boaz, after he lay down at the end of a long day of threshing barley. Lying at his feet, Ruth asked Boaz to cover her with his cloak (Ruth 3:9). Her request for covering was symbolic for seeking protection. Ruth was essentially asking her kinsman redeemer to grant her protection by marrying her and fulfilling his requirement to help her have an heir to carry on her late husband's name. As a foreigner and childless widow, Ruth was an outsider. Others still saw her as the Moabitess, even though she had come back to Bethlehem with Naomi (Ruth 2:6). Boaz, when he first saw her, assumed she was a slave (verse 5). Without children, even the position of honor she once gained as wife of Mahlon would be forgotten.

If we consider the situation through the eyes of the honor-shame worldview, we can see that as an outsider Ruth likely suffered shame, the common verdict for anyone not belonging to the group. But this was not to be Ruth's final story. In a dazzling preview of Christ's mercy, Boaz granted her request for covering and bestowed Ruth with the honor she sought.

Like the literal covering of Adam and Eve, Boaz's covering of Ruth powerfully illustrates the coming of another kinsman redeemer, the Messiah, "born of a woman, born under the law, to redeem those under the law, that we might receive adoption to sonship" (Galatians 4:4-5). Jesus would redeem us by becoming a curse for us (Galatians 3:13-14). He allowed *Himself* to be covered in *our* sin and shame. This is the climax of divine reversal, the holy putting on the unholy so that the unholy might be made holy. He covered His glory so that we might stand uncovered and clean before God.

Second Corinthians 3:18 states beautifully: "We all, who with unveiled faces contemplate the Lord's glory, are being transformed into his image with ever-increasing glory, which comes from the Lord, who is the Spirit." The covered glory of Jesus Christ on the cross has made it possible for us to stand before our Lord, unveiled and reflecting His glory like a pure, beaming bride on her wedding day gazing into the face of her beloved.

Death on a cross was the most shameful form of Roman execution. A man called Rabbi and Lord by His followers, stripped naked and nailed to rough-hewn beams of wood for all to mock, would have from any cultural perspective been horrifically shameful. This is the very reason Muslims argue that if Jesus had indeed been God incarnate, He never would have allowed such humiliation of Himself. But therein lies the wisdom of God that makes foolish the wisdom of man: "For the message of the cross is foolishness to those who are perishing, but to us who are being saved it is the power of God" (1 Corinthians 1:18). Precisely *because* Jesus ultimately covered your shame and mine when He hung naked and exposed on a cross, we can come out of the shadows and live. Shame has been abolished. No manmade method can accomplish this. God, through Jesus Christ, did all of these things, once and for all.

> But God chose the foolish things of the world to shame the wise; God chose the weak things of the world to shame the strong. God chose the lowly things of this world and the despised things—and the things that are not—to nullify the things that are, so that no one may boast before him. It is because of him that you are in Christ Jesus, who has become for us wisdom from God—that is, our righteousness, holiness and redemption (1 Corinthians 1:27-30).

The hollow pride and knowledge of man has been nullified by the One who became for us the very wisdom of God. The Great Coverer, Jesus the Messiah, paid the price for our honor, and we have been redeemed.

THE FINAL PURGE

The last resort, the ultimate sacrifice required to remove our shame, was indeed violent. It involved the death of God Himself, in our stead. The purging of shame came at great cost, not to us, as the honor-shame worldview misguidedly believes, but to God Himself. The next time you see news of an honor killing, cry out to God for the eyes of the Muslim world to be opened to the last resort accomplished for them on Calvary. Shame has been purged for them once and for all. Ask God to help them find the restoration they seek through His Son, Jesus Christ. And if you are carrying shame, avoiding it, covering it, denying it, or considering extreme measures to purge it from your life, may your eyes be opened to the beckoning arms of Christ, who is waiting to take it from you permanently and help you overcome its damaging effects in your life.

THE STRUGGLE IS OVER

The Muslim's struggle to overcome shame is at the heart a human struggle for redemption. The good news of the gospel is that not only are the fearful delivered and the guilty forgiven, but the shamed are given honor. The Messiah has covered Himself in our shame and sin so we no longer have to use man-made methods to handle our brokenness. He has purged once and for all the shame that separated us from God. We do not have to shed blood and commit acts of violence to end the shame. Through faith in the Messiah Jesus, we can stand honored and forgiven before God again.

❧ FOR FURTHER STUDY ❧

1. Read again the account of Adam and Eve's separation from God in Genesis 3:6-10. Underline the words that indicate guilt, shame, and fear.

2. How have you responded to your separation from God? Do you cover up? How are you hiding from Him? Are you afraid of God, and if so, why?

3. Take time to get alone with God and think about your position with Him. Listen for His voice calling you. He is calling you now, just like He did Adam and Eve, asking, "Where are you?" Respond to His call today and let Him restore you. Write a simple prayer below inviting Him to draw near.

8

The Burden Bearers

Because the Sovereign Lord helps me, I will not
be disgraced. Therefore have I set my face like
flint, and I know I will not be put to shame.

ISAIAH 50:7

ome people come into your life and change it forever. This is
what happened to me after I was introduced to Saadiya. The
first day I met her, I had no idea the secrets she carried. I could
not then imagine the joys and sorrows we would one day share or how
close we would become. That first afternoon, as she stood in my living
room, her eyes shyly cast down at the mosaic tile floor, I could not yet
perceive the treasure she was. But God knew. He had always known. In
His great love, He drew her out of shame and showed her how much
He loved her.

When I met Saadiya, she was a single mother living in her father's
home. I learned later that one of the most shameful experiences a Muslim woman in Saadiya's culture can go through is to be rejected by her
husband and sent back to her father's house. The reason for the rejection is not as important as the shame it brings, and the woman bears
the responsibility. Such rejection by her husband not only dishonors the woman and her children, it also dishonors her father and her
extended family. In many cases, families refuse to allow daughters in
these circumstances to reenter their homes.

Saadiya had been young and hopeful once. After completing her

99

education, she secured a respectable position as a bank clerk. She met her husband, and both families agreed the match was strong. The couple was soon married. Saadiya bore two sons, and her position of honor in the family grew. She was doing everything a woman should do to maintain honor in the group according to the conventions of her culture and religion.

Her husband was good to her in the beginning. But shortly after the birth of their second son, he began to drink excessively and abuse Saadiya. The beatings grew more violent, and one day in a rage he grabbed iron rods and tried to blind her. He nearly succeeded. She lost the majority of her sight, severely impairing her ability to do many of the things necessary to keep a house and raise two busy little boys. Shortly after, her husband forced her out of the house with the children.

With nowhere else to go, Saadiya fled to her father's home for refuge. Her elderly, widowed father and disabled brother allowed her to live in their house in exchange for her servanthood. She was relegated to being a slave in her childhood home. Sisters and nieces were not allowed to mention her name or include her in the family circle. Quietly, humbly, she accepted this position of shame.

A few years later, Saadiya gained outside work as a housekeeper. The school fees for her sons were increasing, and she had to find a way to support them. Her father was growing older and more dependent upon her, and her brother's health was declining. Her work as a housekeeper provided just enough for them to get by. But when her husband heard she was working, he appeared demanding money. Although he had taken other wives after expelling Saadiya, he now visited her again, demanding the privileges of a husband in secret. Her shame grew worse. She felt dirty and trapped.

I met her during this time. In the beginning she never spoke of what she suffered, carrying it secretly in her soul like a deserved life sentence. In time, her family and friends began to speak to me about it in hushed whispers. As our relationship grew, Saadiya confided in me and I confided in her. We became like sisters, sharing comfort and sorrow, joy and pain. Saadiya sat with me me during some of the most difficult moments of my life, and I poured endless cups of hot tea as she unburdened her heart to me. We celebrated life together, and I learned from her exquisite humility how to suffer gracefully. Saadiya taught me that no matter where we come from, our hearts are all crafted alike to swell with the changing tides of joy and sorrow. As we lay our delights and our longings down alongside each other's, we experienced the grace and power of God in a mighty way. His love for us did not need explanation in that fragile and brave space.

Eventually Saadiya decided to seek a divorce. This bold move would place her in an all-male court, and the laws of her country state that a woman's testimony is worth only half that of her husband. She would have to testify convincingly to the judge that the abuse she had undergone was just cause for divorce.

Saadiya came to my house on her way to court, breathless and courageous, but also fearful. As my friend looked to me for strength, I took her to the only place I knew to go in such moments. I took her to my Father God and His words. They would tell her what was true about her, no matter what any court decided. We read together these gracious words in Isaiah 54:4-6:

> Do not be afraid; you will not be put to shame. Do not fear disgrace; you will not be humiliated. You will forget the shame of your youth and remember no more the reproach of your widowhood. For your Maker is your husband—the Lord Almighty is his name—the Holy One of Israel is your Redeemer; he is called the God of all the earth. The Lord will call you back as if you were a wife deserted and distressed in spirit—a wife who married young, only to be rejected," says your God.

The words actually shocked me. I could not believe their precise relevance to my friend's situation. As we read the passage together, we both cried. The intimate words were like deep, healing medicine going to the inmost parts of her soul and mine. They showed her, a Muslim woman who had been taught that God was distant and menacing, that she was known by God. They posed the question to me, a Christian woman who trusts that God loves her but often doubts her value: *Do you believe I know you this well?* We both understood in that moment that God loves women everywhere and profoundly understands the issues they face. As we gazed upon His truth together, we received what each of us needed from God. We stood side by side, recipients of His grace and mercy.

I prayed for Saadiya that God would stand with her like a husband in court that afternoon. I boldly asked Him to let her feel His presence in such a powerful way that she knew without doubt that she was not alone. Hers was a complete testimony, with God standing protectively, defensively with her before the judge. I asked Jesus to show her that He is her Redeemer.

The next morning she came running to my house, her face beaming. "He was standing right here!" she exclaimed, patting her right shoulder. "Right *here*! I *knew* God was with me. I was not afraid at all. I did not cry."

The judge granted her freedom from her husband without argument. We danced in circles around my kitchen while the kettle boiled, singing along with us as we praised God. Saadiya encountered our living God through His living Word that day, and so did I. She is now beginning to understand that He loves her and has come to remove her shame.

A PRECARIOUS POSITION

In many parts of the world, especially fundamentalist Islamic societies, honor has been corrupted and distorted. Women are most often its burden bearers in Islamic societies. Instead of bearing the identity of one loved by God, cherished and accepted, women shrink back into the shadows of shame, hidden and exploited. The truth that they are known and valued by God is concealed by the lie that God is a harsh and distant judge, condemning them to a position of lesser worth than their male counterparts.

The responsibility to maintain honor within one's group is a precarious position for women like Saadiya. Circumstances beyond their control can jeopardize family honor, and they are often held accountable for it. For example, the woman who is infertile brings shame to her husband and herself.

In some cultures the language reflects this positional honor or shame—married women who have not borne children are called "little girls," and those who have become mothers are called "women."[1] In many instances, an additional wife is taken with the hope that she will bear children, relegating the first wife to other household duties.

I did not understand the burden women in honor-shame cultures carried when I first began living among them more than 20 years ago. My husband and I had been married three years when we arrived in the remote, dusty village that would be our home for the next two years. We had no children, but our hearts were hopeful and expectant that they would come in due course.

As I learned the language, I began to understand that I was being mocked by the women and children in the village. Neighbor women on their way to the village well would grin bright, toothy smiles behind their hands as they called me "little girl." I thought naively at first it was because I wore my hair in a ponytail with a ribbon. Little did I know it had nothing to do with my hairstyle but everything to do with the fact that I did not have any children. Three years of marriage with no children was a clear conclusion in their culture: I was barren, and my husband needed to do something about it to preserve his honor.

One afternoon as I worked inside our house, a dignified village elder arrived at our door. My husband greeted him and, as was the custom, walked outside with him to talk. After the traditional polite greetings, the old man got down to the real business and purpose of his visit.

"I can see that your wife is a good housewife. I see your laundry hanging out each day, and your front step is clean," he began. My husband nodded and thanked him, expectantly waiting for more. "She is a good housewife," the elder repeated, emphasizing house. "But you have no children." He paused here to hang his head and click sympathetically. "I have a young daughter who is healthy and can give you many children. She is old enough to be married," he continued.

Inside my house, I gasped. By this point I was peeking through the shutters and unabashedly eavesdropping. My Western mind was not used to such a casual conversation about my functions as a wife. I wondered what my husband would say. After a long pause, he replied, "Sir, as a Christian man, I take only one wife."

"But what about your family name?" the elder said. "Who will remember you? You need children to be remembered, to work for you and care for you when you are old. My daughter will give you children, and your first wife can still be in charge of your household."

He waited for my husband to process this before continuing. My husband, on the other hand, was trying to think of how to respectfully bridge the cultural divide and respond in a way that did not insult this respected village elder.

"How many cows did you pay for your wife?" the old man asked.

Here was my husband's opportunity to honorably decline the offer of an additional, "childbearing" wife. "Sir, I am still paying for her," he replied.

The dignified gentleman's eyes grew big with understanding as he exclaimed, sighing with sympathy, "Ohhh! I understand you now."

They continued to talk awhile longer after that, about such things as the crops and the hope for rain. But the subject of my husband's honor in relation to my fertility was not mentioned again. The matter had been closed. My husband obviously could not afford to purchase another wife, regardless of his religious beliefs.

For the two years we lived in that particular village, I never did have a child. We suffered two miscarriages, but it was not until after we moved away that our first son was born. On a regular basis, at night after the village had gone to sleep, women would come to my door shrouded in darkness and visit me. Sitting beside me on the wooden slab that served as our couch, they would pat my leg and lean in close, murmuring, "I understand. I am barren too. We are sisters." Unwittingly I had entered into a sisterhood of burden bearers. Through their eyes, I began to understand only a little the precarious position of women facing circumstances beyond their control, but who nevertheless were responsible for bearing the burden of honor and shame.

DIFFERENT ROLES, SAME NEED

Within the honor-shame system, women and men perform different roles. Women are responsible for training children about what is shameful and how to avoid shame. This is one reason why some Muslim women appear to be promoting the very things Westerners consider oppressive to them, such as the *hijab*, or the extreme and disturbing example of female circumcision, also known as female genital mutilation (FGM).[2]

FGM, which is traditionally thought to reduce a woman's libido, is one way communities seek to ensure marital fidelity. The practice is a social norm in many cultures and is associated with ideas about femininity, including the notion that removal of such organs makes a girl more beautiful and clean, thus increasing her marriageability.[3] As girls, females are taught that they are responsible for the sexual temptations of men. It is shameful to reveal too much skin, for it tempts men, so they must cover themselves. It is shameful to enjoy intercourse, so the organ of enjoyment must be removed. Women teach their daughters what they have been taught: Avoid shame at all costs. This perpetuation of shame instruction can cause females to feel the emotional impact of shame more than men.

Men have an important role in honor-shame training as well. As children grow into preteens and early teenagers, it is the responsibility of men to train them in what is honorable. Women have done their jobs of training in early childhood about what is shameful. Now men continue the training by teaching older children, both boys and girls, what is honorable and how to maintain the honor position.

This is one reason we hear of brothers participating in honor killings after a sister has shamed the family, as in the horrifying case of one brother who shot his sister after she married a non-Muslim.[4] The man who committed this act of violent shame purging is now all alone in prison, his honor stripped rather than restored, as he had hoped and intended.

Stories like these draw an alarming picture of inequality between men and women. As we probe these terrible realities and the impact of honor and shame on Muslim women, we will be tempted to vilify all Muslim men.

Muslim women and Muslim men perform different roles in the

honor-shame paradigm. However, their need for the honor-establish-ing, shame-abolishing gospel of Jesus Christ is identical. Both stand equally loved and valued by God; both stand equally in need of a Sav-ior. We must keep this vital truth in mind as we examine honor and shame in a book intended for a largely female audience. Men, too, feel the impact of shame acutely. The gospel that removes shame is their gospel too. We are all deeply loved and pursued by our Redeemer, no matter our interpretation of the world around us and the means by which we pursue value.

In our human attempt to bring order to our societies that are frag-mented by sin, we create cultural systems. These systems are broken and imperfect. The honor-shame worldview is but one such attempt to make a right path through the wrongness. Like every worldview, it is incomplete. But the good news is that there is One who makes all things complete, has finished the task for us, and invites us to lay our systems at His feet and follow Him as He leads us in a right way.[5] His name is Jesus, and He is the ultimate honor bearer for women from every worldview.

FOR FURTHER STUDY

1. Jesus honored both men and women during His time on earth, and He continues to honor them today. His interactions with both illustrated their equal value and worth in God's eyes. However, His respect and inclusion of women in His ministry was countercultural and controversial at that time. Women were the primary bearers of shame in the culture of Jesus's day, and He understood and addressed this. Read the following New Testament passages and identify in each account the shame the woman carried and how Jesus removed it, giving honor instead.

2. Read Matthew 28:1-10.

   - What shame did the women carry? Hint: In the cultural context of the day, who were the primary authorities and trusted news bearers, women or men?
   - How did Jesus honor the women?

3. Read Luke 13:10-17.

   - What shame did the woman bear?
   - How long had she been unable to stand up straight?
   - Why was the male synagogue ruler indignant?
   - How did Jesus honor the woman?
   - How did Jesus expose shame and restore honor when He responded to the synagogue ruler?
   - Note in 13:17 the responses of the people present. Who was humiliated in the end, and why? Who was delighted, and why?

4. Read Matthew 26:6-13.

   - What shame did the men in Simon's house put upon the woman with the alabaster jar?
   - How did Jesus remove her shame and give her honor instead?

Part Two

Honor
Restored

9

No Longer
Miss the Mark

Return to your fortress, you prisoners of hope; even now
I announce that I will restore twice as much to you.

ZECHARIAH 9:12

One gray afternoon, in a village called Lovely, a woman encountered Jesus the Restorer. Known in Hebrew as Nain, the village was beautifully tucked at the base of a steep mountain. Such a setting was worthy of the name Lovely.

There was nothing lovely about the little town, however, in this woman's mind on this particular day. Her only son was now dead and she was already a widow. Her world had come crashing down around her. No place, no matter its beauty, could restore what her heart had lost. Everything was desolate. The honor she had once known as a wife was a distant memory. The esteem she carried in her community as the mother of a son was now covered in a death shroud, carried to the burial grounds outside the town gate. And what of her future? How long before she followed her husband and son beyond the gate? Disbelief and shock masked her face as she put one heavy foot in front of the other along the narrow mountain road, weeping her way through the nightmare.

> Soon afterward, Jesus went to a town called Nain, and his disciples and a large crowd went along with him. As he

approached the town gate, a dead person was being carried out—the only son of his mother, and she was a widow. And a large crowd from the town was with her. When the Lord saw her, his heart went out to her and he said, "Don't cry." Then he went up and touched the bier they were carrying him on, and the bearers stood still. He said, "Young man, I say to you, get up!" The dead man sat up and began to talk, and Jesus gave him back to his mother (Luke 7:11-14).

What she did not know, what she could not perceive in her state of shock and grief, was that even before the death wail rose from her throat, help was on its way. God Himself was making His way toward her. He who was anointed to preach the good news to the poor would declare news to her that was beyond her wildest imaginings. He who was sent to bind up the brokenhearted, to comfort those who mourn, was at that very moment drawing near to the sorrowful death march. This woman in the city of Lovely would, in mere moments, meet the Savior face-to-face. The day she thought would destroy her future would secure it instead.

In Luke 7:12 we read, "A dead person was being carried out—the *only* son of his mother" (emphasis added). The Greek word here for "only," *monogenēs*, is also used in the Gospel of John to describe Jesus's relationship to God the Father.[1] John, the beloved disciple, used this particular word to illustrate Jesus's complete uniqueness. The word *monogenēs* means one and only, unique. Never before and never again would there be one like Jesus.

Monogenēs is again used in Hebrews 11:17 to describe Isaac during the agonizing obedience of Abraham's willingness to sacrifice his promised son. This highly personal term gives us insight into the deep love God the Father has for His only Son, Jesus Christ. By the same token, it also gives us a deeper understanding of the profound pain God the Father felt when that one-of-a-kind Son, precious and beloved, gave His life to save ours.

This same word, *monogenēs*, is used here in the story of the unnamed widow. A woman who, according to her honor-shame culture, had been stripped of honor and was bereft and desolate. This impactful word is used to describe the son who had died: "As he approached the town gate, a dead person was being carried out—the *monogenēs* [unique, only one of his family] son of his mother, and she was a widow" (Luke 7:12). Then we are told, "When the Lord saw her, his heart went out to her and he said, 'Don't cry'" (verse 13). Such a command on its own might seem cold-hearted. But this was the Lord speaking, the one who would later conquer death on the cross. And this same Lord's "heart went out" to a mourning mother.

I came to better understand this concept in an honor-shame context one day when I, too, was paralyzed by grief. We had lost a child late in pregnancy, and I shut myself in my room for many days. When my dear friend Sana learned of our loss, she came immediately to me and said, "*Bqiti fia, khati. Bqiti fia.*" She mourned with me, for she, too, had known the loss of a child. The Arabic language is poignant and lyrical, much like Hebrew. *Bqiti fi*a means "You stayed within me. Your sorrow and pain lodged itself within me, for it is my pain too." These beautiful words are a deeply personal expression of compassion and empathy and feel like balm to the soul.

I believe that day in the village called Lovely, the pain of a widow lodged itself within the heart of the Savior. It was His pain too. Fully man and fully God, He understood firsthand what that woman felt. He knew the hard obedience that lay before Him as the Son, and He knew the pain it would cause the Father to accomplish eternal restoration for humankind. The Lord understood love and loss. He had the power to comfort and restore the widow of Nain. And that is exactly what He did. The place called Lovely became truly lovely on that afternoon long ago, when a little-known woman, devastated and hopeless, encountered Jesus the Restorer. The crown of beauty, the oil of gladness, and the garment of praise Jesus gave her that day are ours as well. Jesus is a restorer of women's dignity.

GOD'S BURDEN BEARER

Jesus was born into an honor-shame culture. He grew up in an environment preoccupied with honor and shame. Within that context His life and encounters with men and women take on a deeper layer of meaning than most Westerners have ever considered in Sunday school class. His birth itself challenged the conventions of His culture's worldview. From Jesus's conception in the womb of a virgin, God addressed the issue that was foremost on everyone's minds: how to avoid shame.

At the time of Mary's divine visitation, every young Jewish man expected his betrothed to be a virgin. He also anticipated that their union would quickly produce a child. A son to carry on his father's honorable name would be most welcome. Firstborn sons were held in the highest esteem and given authority over younger siblings. Jesus's conception and birth broke all the honor rules of the day. If not for the appearance of the angel of the Lord declaring to Joseph that "what is conceived in her is from the Holy Spirit" (Matthew 1:20), the righteous Israelite never would have taken Mary home as his wife. His assumption through his honor-shame worldview was that Mary was disgraced and unclean because she was pregnant out of wedlock.

Like many men from that worldview still are today, Joseph was preoccupied with avoiding shame, both for himself and Mary. Without God's intervention, Joseph would have followed the dictates of his culture, avoiding shame by divorcing her quietly (Matthew 1:19). As it happened, Joseph married a virgin and gained a son who would carry on His heavenly Father's name for eternity.

The Jewish people were also intimately familiar with the concept of burden bearing in relationship to sin and shame. Old Testament law taught them the necessity of a burden bearer, a sacrificial animal that would serve as a substitute for the people, bearing the penalty of their sin. In Hebrew, this was called an *azazel*. In modern English, we translate it "scapegoat." Azazel literally meant "goat of removal."[2] According to *Easton's Bible Dictionary*, the form of this word signifies the total separation of sin from the people: It was wholly carried away.[3] The visible demonstration of the scapegoat being sent into the wilderness, outside the camp, emphasized the validity of the transaction.

On the Day of Atonement, the most holy day of worship in the Hebrew calendar, the high priest performed two vital ceremonies, involving two goats: One would perish and one would live (Leviticus 16:7-10). The purpose was also twofold: to make the people clean before the Lord and to remove their sins. The first goat was sacrificial; the second was the scapegoat.

First, the high priest killed the sacrificial goat, taking its blood into the center of the most holy place in the tabernacle. There the blood was sprinkled on the altar, symbolically cleansing God's people, the high priest, and the sanctuary. After that, the high priest placed his hands on the head of the scapegoat and confessed the sins of Israel, symbolically transferring those sins to the living animal. The scapegoat was then taken deep into the wilderness, far outside the camp or city, and released, as an illustration of the people's sin and shame literally being carried away.

This elaborate Levitical ceremony served the purpose of making God's people clean before Him. In chapter 3, we discussed that *clean* is one of the many synonyms for "honored." *Dirty* is another word for ashamed or sinful. God provided a way to become clean again for His people who had been dishonored and dirtied by sin and shame. The process involved sacrifice and burden bearing.

Jesus embodied both the sacrificial animal and the scapegoat. Through His blood He provided atonement or cleansing from sin for every person. As a result, we can now enter the most holy place and we are eternally redeemed (Hebrews 9:11-12). Christ was crucified outside the walls of the city, His death a spectacle of shame in the culture of His time. Like the scapegoat, His death is a visible demonstration of the complete removal of our sin and shame.

God is patient. He sent His Son, Jesus, to be both the sacrifice that would make us eternally clean before God and the scapegoat who would bear our shame and sin upon Himself, away from us forever. This is God's provision and the only way of redemption for every person.

> Come to me, all you who are weary and heavy laden, and I will give you rest. Take my yoke upon you and learn from me, for I am gentle and humble in heart, and you will find rest for your souls. For my yoke is easy and my burden is light (Matthew 11:28-30).

Pray that Muslims around the world will hear this gentle invitation and lay their burdens at the feet of God's burden bearer, Jesus Christ. May they exchange the yoke of religious rules for the rest He offers. He has already taken the disgrace far from us, making a way for us to stand clean before God for eternity.

GOD'S CHOSEN LIBERATOR

Jesus was fully aware of the burdens women carried in their efforts to avoid shame and maintain honor, and He addressed them with truth, compassion, and mercy. In His time here on earth, Jesus was deliberate and intentional in His interactions with women. He was making a statement about freedom and equality. He was also leaving for us a carefully drawn map that we might be able to navigate the very character of God regarding the issue of women in society.

Jesus was a liberator of women, and He remains so today. The Lord's emancipation of the oppressed and overpowered is beautifully described in Psalm 18.

> He reached down from on high and took hold of me; he drew me out of deep waters. He rescued me from my powerful enemy, from my foes, who were too strong for me. They confronted me in the day of my disaster, but the LORD was my support. He brought me out into a spacious place; he rescued me because he delighted in me (verses 16-19).

The well-known story of the adulterous woman in John 8:3-11 is one such occasion where a woman found herself in deep waters, confronted and condemned. Found with a man who was not her husband, she had been violently dragged by the religious leaders to the public square. We learn that she had been caught in the act of adultery, which, according to the law of that time, placed her in a clear position of shame and an expected death sentence.

Thrown to the ground by her accusers, she was filthy, humiliated, and completely exposed. More exposed, in fact, than even she realized. For the man in front of whom they had forced her was God Himself. Standing before her was a man who would within a short time bear her shame and sin on the cross. Of course, no one had any idea.

We have commonly read this story with an emphasis on the hypocrisy of the religious leaders of the day. Now when I read it, I see a story of shame exposed and its bearer redeemed. Intending to trap Him, the teachers of the law and Pharisees brought what they considered a clear case of legal and moral wrongdoing before Jesus. Religious law of the day demanded indictment of one caught in adultery. Had they known that the One they asked to judge was *the* Judge, the Rescuer, the Lord spoken of in Psalm 18 above, which they all surely knew by heart, they would have trembled in fear and shame and joined the condemned woman on the ground in humiliation and repentance.

But they did not. They were operating within their broken system of rules, distorted by humankind.

> [They] said to Jesus, "Teacher, this woman was caught in the act of adultery. In the Law Moses commanded us to stone such women. Now what do you say?" They were using this question as a trap, in order to have a basis for accusing him. But Jesus bent down and started to write on the ground with his finger. When they kept on questioning him, he straightened up and said to them, "Let any one of you who is without sin be the first to throw a stone at her." Again he stooped down and wrote on the ground. At this, those who heard began to go away one at a time, the older ones first, until only Jesus was left, with the woman still standing there (John 8:4-9).

"If any of you is without sin…" Only one in the temple courts that day stood sinless, and it was the Savior Himself. The manner in which Jesus confronted them spoke of their equality before God. Accuser and accused, the men and the woman, condemned. Accuser and accused, the men and the woman, in need of a Messiah to save them. None of them able to redeem themselves by their good works.

The air, which moments before quivered with anger and rage, grew still and silent as those religious men let Jesus's words sink in. Starting with the oldest and wisest, they responded with honesty. They could not deny their own shame. So they left the scene, carrying their burdens with them, away from the One who could have released their souls' struggle against sin.

The condemned woman's encounter with Jesus draws a poignant picture of how He deals with our shame. Among its other lies, shame tells us that because we bear it, we are less valuable than others. This belief has led many to despair of life itself. I wonder how the woman felt as she watched the men leave. Was she in despair, expecting death at the hands of the remaining man before her? She must have been astonished and bewildered as her accusers crept away one by one, leaving her crouching there, dirty before Jesus. If this man had the humble audacity to confront her critics, *what else might He do?* She was riveted in place by a rare mix of shame and curiosity, despair and hope. I wonder what went through her mind.

> "Woman, where are they? Has no one condemned you?"
> "No one, sir," she said. "Then neither do I condemn you," Jesus declared. "Go now and leave your life of sin" (John 8:10-11).

"Leave your life of sin." The Greek says it this way: "Go now and *mēketi*[4] (no longer) *hamartane*[5] (miss the mark in your relationship to God)."

The woman thrown at Jesus's feet lived in a culture where righteousness was determined by how well one followed religious rules. This was no easy feat for any person. In the years since the Ten Commandments were given to Moses, Jewish leaders had added many additional, tedious rules. For example, the fourth commandment was to "Remember the Sabbath day by keeping it holy" (Exodus 20:8). Essentially this meant Jews were not to work on the Sabbath. The Pharisees added 39 separate categories to define *work*, and within each were subcategories.[6] One's standing before God depended on adherence to the rules.

Similarly in Islam, righteousness, or acceptance, before God depends on how well one follows the rules. If good behaviors outweigh bad, the Muslim *may* attain God's approval. Like the accused Jewish woman in John 8, many Muslim women today live their lives wondering if they can ever hit the mark in their relationship to God.

I wish every Muslim woman could listen in on Jesus's conversation with the adulteress that day. He peered straight into her thoughts and responded as if they were talking out loud about her innermost fears.

No longer miss the mark.

In that moment, she knew she was standing before God Himself. He set her free from shame. He was the guarantee that she would never miss the mark again.

Alone with the Savior, the woman was not further berated and abused. Rather, she was forgiven and restored, instructed and liberated. She left the place of humiliation with a new life sparkling with hope and value. She surely never expected that outcome in the terrible moments when she was seized and taken to the public square.

Examining this passage through the lenses of honor and shame challenges me. I am a follower of Christ. I have accepted His lordship over my life and the forgiveness of my sins. But have I fully understood that He also removes *my* secret shame? Am I still striving to hit the mark with my perfectionism or my performance? As I learn more about the burden my Muslim friends carry, I learn more about my own cumbersome load. The answer for both of us is one and the same: God's chosen liberator, Jesus Christ. Jesus is the restorer of honor for every woman in every culture.

❧ FOR FURTHER STUDY ❧

1. Read again the opening passage of this chapter, Zechariah 9:12.

   - What does it mean to be a "prisoner of hope"?

   - Who or what is the fortress referred to in this passage?

2. Read Joel 3:16. Underline the words that describe the Lord as a fortress. Have you trusted Him as your fortress? Have you become a "prisoner of hope"? You can do so today. Write a prayer below, asking God to be your fortress and give you hope.

3. Read Romans 4:18-21. God has promised honor instead of shame to those who will place their faith in Him.

   - What shame stood between Abraham and God's honor promises?

   - What role did hope play in Abraham's life?

   - What was the result?

Right There All Along

What is mankind that you are mindful of them, human
beings that you care for them? You have made them
a little lower than the angels and crowned them with
glory and honor. You made them rulers over the works
of your hands; you put everything under their feet.

PSALM 8:4-6

Those with a Western worldview read the Bible with a focus on sin and forgiveness. Because of that mind-set, shame and honor in the Old and New Testaments are commonly overlooked. Honor-shame language is ubiquitous in the Bible, but we often skim right over it. Words such as *shame, disgrace, glory, honor, reputation, name, worthy, stranger, poor,* and many others reveal honor's and shame's centrality to the biblical context and narrative. Learning to recognize not only sin and forgiveness in the Bible but also shame and honor will transform how we perceive and relate to those from an honor-shame worldview, as well as change the way we look at ourselves.

Many people who fill the seats of Western churches today readily agree that they have been forgiven through Jesus Christ. Yet they carry the weight of shame, hidden from view, and do not know how to escape its condemnation. Shame is choking the Western church, yet the gospel addresses it fully, if we only have eyes to see it.

COVERED FROM THE START

We already discussed shame's debut upon the stage of humanity.

After their disobedience, Adam and Eve realized they were naked and hid from God. Not wanting to be seen, they sewed fig leaves to cover their nakedness. Shame burned its way through their hearts as man and woman tried in vain to cover their sense of unworthiness. Humanity has been pursuing this goal ever since. Today we cover our shame in the neatly stitched garments of good works, Facebook friends, or health obsessions. No matter what we sew together and hide behind, we are still trying to keep ourselves from truly being seen and possibly rejected.

Adam and Eve were not only guilty of disobedience, they were also then shameful before God. Humiliation was not merely an emotion they felt in response to their sin: Humiliation was a fact that changed their position in relationship to God. Sin led to shame. Disobedience led to separation from God. The honored status bestowed upon Adam and Eve at creation was lost when a curse took its place. As a result, they would experience pain, hard work, hunger, and weakness, all signs of their new dishonored status. Their disgrace led to the disgrace of all mankind.

God, in His mercy, provided covering for their shame. Blood was shed for the first time, and animal skins would cover Adam and Eve's nakedness. This powerful picture of the coming Messiah, who would shed His blood to cover the disgrace of man and woman, is given to us from the start of God's great narrative so that we might have hope. God will provide a way out of our sin and shame. The story is not over when we seem to have destroyed everything. *There is hope.*

THE SUFFERING SERVANT

Christ's purpose was not only to forgive sin but also to display God's honor. *Honor* is another word for glory. Every time we see *glory* in the Bible, a bell should ring in our minds, declaring the honor of God. The Old Testament often uses the Hebrew word *kābôd* to describe the glory and honor of God, for the word embodies both meanings.[1] A beautiful example is found in Exodus 29:43, describing the beauty of God's meeting place with His people at the entrance to the Tent of Meeting: "There also I will meet with the Israelites, and the place will be consecrated by my glory."

In the New Testament, the Greek word *doxa* is an example of another word meaning both glory and honor. Luke used it in 9:32 to describe how Jesus appeared to Peter and his companions at the transfiguration. In this passage, it denotes the shining forth of a person and is used particularly of God, equivalent to *kābôd*.[2] Jesus was sinless, and He suffered God's wrath to achieve for us the forgiveness of sins. Fully God and fully man, He endured shame and was given honor by the Father so He could display the glory of God.

We may be uncomfortable with the image of the Lord's servant who had no beauty or majesty, nothing in His appearance that we should desire (Isaiah 53:2). Perhaps we cannot quite understand a God who was despised and rejected by men, a man of sorrows familiar with suffering. Like one from whom men hide their faces, Jesus was despised and not esteemed (verse 3). But this is the One foreshadowed from the beginning, as Adam and Eve stood ashamed and suffering before their merciful Creator. He was coming even then, from the start, to bring humanity back home to God. He would take up their infirmities and carry their sorrows. He would be crushed for their iniquities, and the punishment brought upon Him would bring all men and women peace. By His wounds they would be healed (verses 4-5). Finally, after the suffering of His soul, the servant of the Lord would see the light of life and be satisfied (verse 11). The glory and honor of God lies in His great, rescuing love of you and me. It has been displayed since the beginning and will bear us up to the end.

THE GOSPEL OF OPPOSITES

As stated above, Jesus was born into an honor-shame culture, and the gospel was accomplished within it. Emmanuel, God with us, left His place of honor to enter a world of man-made systems and distorted value. The honor-shame worldview is but one man-made system, imperfect and incomplete. Because the biblical writers were looking through honor-shame lenses, however, they saw no need to explain social values such as family, hospitality, community, ethnicity, and respect for elders. These values were intrinsic to honor-shame culture, and the biblical authors intuitively understood them. When modern readers now examine the ancient texts, they are influenced by Western values such as individuality, rationalism, legality, and egalitarianism, resulting in what Jayson Georges calls "cultural blindness."[3] Our understanding of the biblical texts is directly influenced by our culture and its values.

What I find fascinating is that, although the long-awaited Messiah was born into an honor-shame culture, what He did was absolutely contrary to that culture's understanding of the world and the Savior who would one day come to rescue them. From an honor viewpoint, the one true God, mighty and powerful, merciful and just, would never allow Himself to be shamed. He would never lay aside His majesty for the wooden cross of a criminal, dying in the place of a murderer. The One whom psalmists sang of giving life (Psalm 21:4; 91:16; 103:4) would never die the death of a life-taker.

Muslims hold the view that God would never permit Himself to be shamed so completely, and they take great issue with the thought that Jesus, whom they believe to be an honored prophet of God, would suffer such humiliating defeat. Was God not able to protect His prophet? Would that not bring shame to God? Along this line of logic, the Christian insistence that Jesus died on the cross is itself proof to Muslims that Jesus was not God. Islamic scholars give various explanations for what exactly happened to Jesus on the day of the crucifixion. Some teach that He was lifted up to heaven to escape persecution. Another Islamic tradition teaches that someone else died in His place, allowing His followers to secretly take Him away. The Qur'an itself states clearly "for of a surety they killed him (Jesus) not" (4:157-59).[4] Islam's adamant insistence on an alternate crucifixion narrative reflects the cultural view that one must avoid shame at all costs. Especially if that one is God. So they labor in a system not unlike Old Testament law, heaving the weight of sin and shame upon their own shoulders, trying to follow the rules, wearying themselves in an effort to be right, honorable, and accepted by God.

But Jesus had a habit of turning human customs and beliefs upside down and inside out, forcing humanity out of its stifled and limited way of thinking. The gospel is a message of humility and servanthood made evident in the life of God Himself as He laid aside His rights and chose obedience to a suffering He did not deserve, to rescue a people who deserved death instead of mercy.

> Let the same mind be in you that was in Christ Jesus, who, though he was in the form of God, did not regard equality with God as something to be exploited, but emptied himself, taking the form of a slave, being born in human likeness. And being found in human form, he humbled himself and became obedient to the point of death—even death on a cross. Therefore God also highly exalted him and gave him the name that is above every name (Philippians 2:5-9 NRSV).

The mystery of the gospel of opposites leaves us speechless. We fall on our knees in awe of Jesus, the One who bears the name that is above every name. God has done for us what we could not accomplish for ourselves, no matter our worldview. He has forgiven our sins, restored our honor, and given us power over fear. The upside-down gospel speaks into all worldviews and leads us in a right way.

JESUS'S HONOR PRAYER

Jesus openly prayed about His glory, the glory given to Him by the Father so that He in turn gives it to everyone who believes in Him. The Greek word *doxa* is once again used here to describe Jesus's glory. But Jesus took it a step further and asked the Father to give that *doxa* to those who believe in Him. When used to describe believers in Christ, the word signifies a state in which they are accorded the fullest enjoyment of the admiration and honor of God—the object of His highest regard and praise.[5] This is astounding. God now gives His children the full admiration, honor, regard, and praise reserved for His Son, Jesus. Jesus had a right to that glory. In God's mysterious love, He extended that right to us through Jesus's sacrifice.

The circle has closed. Man and woman began in a position of honor, enjoying mutual, reciprocal admiration and love in a secure relationship with God. Sin brought shame and severed that relationship, separating humanity from intimacy with God. God sent His Son, Jesus, to bear the shame and sin, abolishing it forever for those who would believe in Him.

In the Gospel of John we are privileged to eavesdrop on one of the most astonishing prayers ever prayed. The Rescuer was closing the loop, once again interceding for broken humanity so that they may believe that God has loved them since before the creation of the world. Jesus has restored honor and made unity with God and each other possible once again.

> I pray also for those who will believe in me through their [the disciples'] message, that all of them may be one, Father, just as you are in me and I am in you. May they also be in us so that the world may believe that you have sent me. I have given them the glory that you gave me, that they may be one as we are one—I in them and you in me—so that they may they be brought to complete unity. Then the world will know that you sent me and have loved them even as you have loved me. Father, I want those you have given me to be with me where I am, and to see my glory, the glory you have given me because you loved me before the creation of the world (17:20-24).

This passage is eye-opening to the glorious purpose for which Jesus came. What we know is that the Father loved Him and glorified Him. What we might not know is that God offers to us the exact same esteem, honor, and love that He gave to Jesus.

One morning my husband and I were driving through a small English village on our way to morning seminary classes where we were studying missiology and cultural anthropology. Through the car window I saw a flash of lovely lilac purple. It's my favorite color, and it drew my gaze immediately. A little girl was wearing a lilac coat as she walked to school. Her small hand was clasped firmly by the large, strong hand of her father. He looked down at her with love and laughter, and she returned his look of affection with chattered words I could not hear.

The pair was a charming sight. But deep in my heart, in the hidden place where we hide our shame, I felt a piercing pain. I have always wanted a father. Not knowing mine has been one of my life's great losses. Even as a grown woman, the grief catches me unawares, reminding me that I grew up fatherless. As I looked out at the girl and her daddy, I wished I were the one walking down the street, holding my father's strong, safe hand, basking in his delight as I wore a lovely lilac coat.

Over the years, my Father God has taken my hand in His strong, safe one, looked upon me with delight, and listened for hours to my chatter. That little English girl so long ago had a right to be loved and adored by her father. She was his own daughter. I know now that because of Jesus, I have a right to be loved and adored by my Father God as well, for I am His own daughter.

No matter our story, our worldview, or our culture, we have been offered the right to become God's own children, enjoying the full admiration, love, and delight of His Father heart. We no longer stand apart, alone, insecure, or unsafe. Jesus asked His Father to help us believe it is true and accept His gift of restoration.

BRIMMING OVER

Understanding that the Bible is brimming with honor themes will change our lives. We will discover something missing in our relationship with God and each other, and our hearts will weigh less as we lay shame aside. In later chapters, we will examine how to understand the gospel through the honor-shame framework so that we can share it from that worldview with those who are in our lives. But we must first understand it ourselves and closely inspect the unaddressed shame in our lives. As we begin to comprehend how deep and how wide is the love and honor bestowed upon us by the Father, our testimony will flow naturally out of us, drawing others to this life-changing truth.

❧ FOR FURTHER STUDY ❧

In this chapter we have learned that the themes of honor and shame are found throughout the Old and New Testaments. Examine the following well-known passages for honor-shame themes. Underline any honor or shame vocabulary you find.

1. Read Genesis 6:5-10,18. In this passage, we learn that mankind can shame God.[6]

   • Describe mankind's actions, according to Genesis 6:5.

   • The behavior of humanity dishonored God and His creation. God's heart was filled with great pain and grief, and He was sorry He had made people. However, there was one man who honored God, and whom God honored in return. Their relationship of mutual honor prevented the complete destruction of humanity. Who was this man?

2. Read Psalm 62:7.

   • What is the source of all honor for women and men?

   • On whom do we depend for our value?

   • What promises are illustrated by the metaphors "rock" and "refuge" in this passage?

3. Read John 1:12-14.

   • In what must we believe in order to become children of God?

   • Why is the name so important?[7]

   • By whose authority do we gain the right to be children of God?

Instead of Hidden, Seen

You have searched me, Lord, and you know me.

PSALM 139:1

Arresting in their beauty, her brown eyes were gracefully framed by long eyelashes and a carefully drawn line of kohl along the upper lids. I momentarily forgot I was at a surgical clinic to repair facial deformities. I saw no deformity in this beautiful young woman. But she had not yet removed the cobalt-blue scarf that draped over her hair and face, hiding her complete visage from view. I offered her a chair as I closed the door to my office. Most examinations were done in the open area of the lobby where children and adults with cleft lips and palates all clamored to get their names on the priority list. Shame about their condition was something they had left behind in their villages and cities. Now hope gusted through the motley crowd instead, punctuated by occasional outbursts of laughter or games of tag among the little ones. Today was a day of excitement and nervousness as people, dusty from their brave journeys, patiently anticipated the possibility of repair and new smiles.

By contrast, the woman in the striking blue scarf made a beeline for me through the bustling crowd and spoke in hushed tones. I leaned close to make out her request. "Peace be upon you and may God give long life to your parents," she said in greeting. "Could you have mercy on me and see me alone?" I sensed the shame and urgency in her manner. She held the posture of one who was risking everything, precariously balanced on the razor-sharp edge of despair and hope. I asked a colleague to cover me while I led her to a private space where we could speak without an audience.

Now here we were, alone in a room, her beautiful eyes looking straight at me as though measuring my trustworthiness. To break the ice, I began with customary, polite questions.

"Have you traveled far?"

"Yes. My village is many hours from here."

"What is your name?"

"Jameelah."

"You must be tired. May I get you a glass of water?"

"No, thank you."

I waited, saying a silent prayer that God would give me wisdom to know best how to assist Jameelah and to help her trust me.

"I am not like the people out there," she finally said, gesturing beyond the closed door.

"I was born complete, without any deformity. My father has been fiercely protective of me. He would not let men see my face because he did not want unworthy ones asking for my hand in marriage. He told me to wait and one day he would find the right husband for me. Father did find a man for me eventually, but he was as old as my father and I was not pleased with him. He came to our home and brought gold necklaces and beautiful dresses, but I was not impressed with his old face and wrinkled hands. I met a boy at school whom I loved, and I wanted to marry him." Jameelah paused here, nervously readjusting her scarf with henna-tipped fingers, making sure only her eyes were visible.

"Father and I had many fights about this. I cried and begged him not to make me marry the old man. When the old man came one day with sweets and perfume, I threw them at him and told him I would not marry him because I was in love with a handsome boy my own age. This humiliated my father, and my mother ran to her room weeping. The next week, as I was carrying food to the animals, a man with a covered face leapt out of the bushes with a machete and destroyed my beauty. He said, 'If I cannot have you, no one will.' He left me lying on the ground bleeding, until I passed out. When I woke up, I was in my bed. My mother and my aunts took care of me until the wound closed."

She stopped here and carefully removed her scarf. I had been trained to maintain my composure when working with those who have severe facial deformities. But in that moment, it was extremely difficult to withhold my distress at what had been done to this exquisitely lovely young woman. The face looking back at me appeared to be the image of a broken mirror. A jagged line ran from the top right corner of her cheekbone, across her nose, and down to the far edge of her opposite jawbone, creating a ghastly asymmetry of what had once been a perfectly balanced face. Jameelah's full lips were separated by a rutted purple ridge, the thick scar tissue making some sounds difficult to form as she spoke.

I let my eyes fill with the tears that demanded to flow. Reaching out my right hand, I took hers and murmured Arabic expressions of sorrow and disbelief. Her bravely squared shoulders relaxed and she leaned closer. "I know God sees me. Can you help me?"

✥

We are not unlike the girl with a face like the image of a broken mirror. Who we were originally designed to be, our true image, is distorted to us. The archetype of humanity has been disfigured by sin and shame. The unblemished beauty of God's original creation has been marred. But God sees us, and help is here.

A wonderful Greek term, *paraklēsis*,[1] used in the Bible, describes the ministry of the Holy Spirit. Paraklēsis is the ministry of coming alongside that the Spirit of God provides us: helping, comforting, understanding, counseling, and strengthening us. Jesus called the Holy Spirit the "Paraclete," or helper (John 14:16). The Holy Spirit helps us understand who we were created to be. He reveals to us our true worth and identity, and He aids our understanding of the honor that is rightfully ours as children of God.

In the same way that He helps us in our own struggle to see clearly who we are in Christ, we have the opportunity to come alongside and help Muslim women. We lay down our own pain, our joys, our common experiences of womanhood alongside theirs and recognize our common need for a rescuer, the Lord Jesus. It is in this paraclete ministry that we see God's power to open a closed heart and give sight to blind eyes.

This ministry is not really possible, though, until we first understand our own need to be seen. We cannot minister effectively until we grapple with our own distorted image and our own need for the God who sees us. How can we declare honor and value to others if we have not fully believed and accepted it in our own lives?

HAGAR'S STORY

In the book of Genesis, at the beginning of God's story of love for us, we find an astonishing example of God's rescuing love for a woman in desperate circumstances. She was a woman hidden from view, cast out of her tribe and nation, made a slave in the house of foreigners and, eventually, expelled from that household.

The story of this woman, who would become the mother of the nation of people we now know as Muslims, is found in Genesis 16. Her name, Hagar, means "to flee." The Arabic word for Hagar is *Hajar*, and it has become a common female name in some parts of the Muslim world. Its Arabic root, *hijrah*, describes the migration of early Muslims from Mecca to Medina in 622 AD.[2] Seventh-century Muslims were not simply migrating; they were fleeing. Fleeing from persecution, harm, and oppression; seeking peace, safety, freedom, and justice. *Hijrah* is still happening today as Muslim refugees escape from their homelands by the hundreds of thousands, seeking the same things. In modern Arabic, *hijrah* has been used to describe uprooting, hurried departure that does not even allow people to take their belongings with them, abandoning and forsaking homes, communities, and nations. It implies leaving one's home and becoming a foreigner in a strange land, even forced homelessness. *Hijrah* means a breaking of relationships, a profound change in one's entire life systems.

I find it fascinating to think that this woman and her story right here in Genesis so widely influenced the Islamic culture we know today.

The story of Hagar is given in significant detail in the major *hadith* collection *Sahih al-Bukhari*.³ Hagar's exile in the desert is central to the sacred pilgrimage to Mecca (*hajj*) each Muslim must make once in his or her lifetime. During their journey, pilgrims pay homage to Hagar by walking or running between the points symbolizing the Marwa and Safa mountains, the same path Hagar purportedly took according to the hadith.⁴

In the Genesis account, Hagar was a servant to Sarai, the wife of the man we now know as Abraham, the name God later gave him. But while he was still called Abram, he was promised by God that he would have a son and that his descendants would be as numerous as the stars in the sky. Time passed and Sarai did not conceive. So Sarai proposed that Abram sleep with her maidservant, Hagar, and build a family through her.

Remember, honor-shame culture is collectivist, and Hagar's story takes place in an honor-shame society. A person's identity was strongly attached to membership in one's group, and priority was placed on group over self. Because of what we have learned about the honor-shame context in which Hagar and Sarai lived, we can surmise that Hagar had already experienced the loss of her position in her original group; when she left Egypt, she lost her place among her family, her community, and her nation. Removal from the group equals shame in the honor-shame paradigm.

Hagar was already living a life shadowed by shame as an outsider in a family, a community, and a nation not her own. When commanded to sleep with her master, Hagar likely had to negotiate the lesser shame. Shame-sufferers have keen survival instincts. On the one hand was the shame that would result from losing her virginity, her marriage equity. On the other hand was the possibility of honor that would come with bearing her master the long-desired and promised son. As Sarai's servant, she knew about God's famous promise to Abram. She also observed Sarai's consequent impatience and despair as, month after month, her barrenness was displayed. Hagar possibly saw an opportunity to redeem herself, to remove some of her own shame through her union with Abraham.

When Hagar became pregnant, she must have thought she had succeeded. She became even more determined in her pursuit of shame removal. Did hatred for Sarai grow in Hagar's heart? Did she dream of supplanting her? We don't know for sure, but we do know that Hagar despised Sarai (Genesis 16:4). In turn, Sarai blocked Hagar's only way of redeeming herself from shame. Sarai complained to Abram and told him that he was responsible for the problem now looming between her and her servant. He then gave Sarai authority to do whatever she wanted with Hagar. Her response was to oppress Hagar, making her life unbearable. Hagar ran away, marking the first recorded *hijrah* in Muslim history.

This is when we find Hagar alone and on the brink of an encounter with God that would change her life.

> The angel of the LORD found Hagar near a spring in the desert; it was the spring that is beside the road to Shur. And he said, "Hagar, slave of Sarai, where have you come from, and where are you going?" "I'm running away from my mistress Sarai," she answered (Genesis 16:7-8).

The Lord found Hagar near a spring. In Hebrew, the word for spring is *'ayin*.[5] We discussed in chapter 3 that in Arabic, Hebrew's linguistic cousin, the word *'ayin* also exists but with a small difference in pronunciation. In both languages, the word has the same two primary meanings: It is defined as eye, vision, or eyesight, and spring.[6]

In the Arab country where I once lived for many years, I learned that in colloquial Arabic, *'ayin* has a third important meaning. It is also the source from which your family "springs." Today the word is commonly used to describe one's character, the quality of one's family, and the honor or shame for which that family is known.

The first time I understood this meaning clearly was in the market one day after I resisted the marriage proposal of a man who had been persistently following me. In angry response to my refusal, he sought to shame me in the street, shouting loudly, "It is better anyway for a man to find a wife from his own *'ayin* (spring)!" In other words, his race and family were superior to mine anyway; therefore, it was more honorable for him to seek marriage from within his own family rather than outside. To cover the shame my rejection caused him, the man publicly called out my position. The crowds gawked at me, and old ladies behind *niqabs* (veils that cover the lower face, allowing the eyes to peek out) tsk-tsked, shaking their heads derisively. *'Ayin*, or spring, can symbolize one's deepest identity, one's source of life. I was an outsider. I was ranked shameful on the street that day for refusing my chance to become an insider by marriage.[7] The source from which I sprang proved it.

We read in Jeremiah 2:13 that God is our *'ayin*. He is our spring of living water, our source of life, identity, and value. No other spring can fully validate our worth. "My people have committed two sins: They have forsaken me, the spring of living water, and have dug their own cisterns, broken cisterns that cannot hold water." Isaiah also used imagery of a spring, or well, of life-giving water to describe the source of life and salvation. Not only is God the source of our life; He also is the source of our strength, our defense, and our rescue.

> "Surely God is my salvation; I will trust and not be afraid. The LORD, the LORD himself, is my strength and my defense; he has become my salvation." With joy you will draw water from the wells of salvation (Isaiah 12:2-3).

One day Jesus intentionally rerouted His journey to Galilee to sit awhile and chat with an outcast woman in Samaria. She was living in shame and isolation from her community, forced to come to the village well at the hottest time of the day when no one else would be there. In this way she could avoid those who might jeer at her and criticize her for the wrong choices she had made in life. Jesus, during His encounter with her, used the metaphor of a spring to help her understand that He was the source of eternal life.

> Jesus answered, "Everyone who drinks this water will be thirsty again, but whoever drinks the water I give them will never thirst. Indeed, the water I give them will become in them a spring of water welling up to eternal life" (John 4:13-14).

Long before Jesus sat down to wait by the village spring in Samaria, God waited by a spring in the desert along another dusty road. To really grasp Hagar's experience with God, we must understand the crucial significance of the spring and the source of life. "The angel of the LORD found Hagar near a spring in the desert; it was the spring that is beside the road to Shur" (Genesis 16:7). Hagar was in a very real sense having an identity crisis. She had unwittingly drawn near the Source, the Spring of Life, the Creator God Himself. When God found her, Hagar was *near* the spring, not quite *at* it. If we examine this moment through the lenses of honor and shame, we might even say that without honor or family, Hagar was searching for herself, for meaning in her life, for *identity*. Hagar had no idea how *near* she was to the Source of all life, to an identity change that would impact all generations after her, including the Muslims you and I know.

If we read this passage allegorically, we can see ourselves on the journey from shame to honor. How good of the Lord to find us in our search, before we have even quite made it to our goal. His eyes see our pursuit of identity, and He meets us along the way. This is what He did for Hagar, and what He continues to do today for women everywhere.

Hagar's desert spring was beside the road to Shur. *Road* in Genesis 16:7 in Hebrew is *derek*, a word that can also mean "way of life, lot in life."[8] Hagar was doing what she had always done, her way of life, her lot in life, which for her was *running away*. That was, after all, what her name meant. She believed it was her identity.

God's question, "Where have you come from, and where are you going?" in verse 8 was a challenge. If God ever asks that question, get ready. He already knows where you and I have come from and where we are planning to go. He asked Adam and Eve a similar question framed in similar language when they were hiding from Him after eating the forbidden fruit. This revealing question is not intended to expose the answer to the Asker, but rather to reveal the truth to the one being asked. Something had blinded Hagar's heart. When God asked, "Where have you come from, and where are you going?" she answered truthfully, "I am running away." It was as if her bare statement of fact was also an honest confession: "I can't take it anymore."

Then the angel of the LORD told her, "Go back to your mistress and submit to her." The angel added, "I will increase your descendants so much that they will be too numerous to count." The angel of the LORD also said to her: "You are now pregnant and you will give birth to a son. You shall name him Ishmael, for the LORD has heard of your misery" (Genesis 16:9-11).

In the United States, it has become popular in recent years for expectant parents to have a "gender reveal party" where the proud mother and father announce to friends and family the gender of the coming baby. What an astonishing gender-reveal party Hagar had there on a dusty roadside with the angel of the Lord! God Himself told Hagar what was true about her, what she did not even know about herself. She was having a boy, ensuring her honor for all the generations to come.

In this passage, God answered Hagar's real need. God did not address how stressed out she was about Sarai's mistreatment of her. God did not attend to the matter of how unfair it all was that she had been used. Instead, God answered the pivotal question at the heart of the matter, the question of who Hagar was in relation to God. She might not even have been fully aware of that need, but God knew that every other need in her life depended on that one being met. It is the same for us today. If we do not know who we are in relation to God, our other needs cannot be completely met.

In Old Testament times a person's relationship with God was defined in terms of obedience or disobedience. God gave Hagar a command to obey, but He did not stop there. He gave her a command, and He gave her *helpers*. Hagar needed help to obey this command and change the entire course of her life. Have you ever felt that way? You have heard a command from God, but you need a little help obeying it. The good news is that God never leaves us helpless. He actually provides us help to obey. That is exactly what He did for Hagar. Hagar's helpers were called Hope and a Future—the same help He would promise to exiled Israelites a thousand years later (Jeremiah 29:11), and the same help He promises His children today. Furthermore, and perhaps most reassuring, He promised His own presence with her. The name of the son she carried was to be Ishmael, meaning "God, He heard me!"[9]

After God gave Hagar a preview of her future, something astonishing happened. Hagar's shame was removed. She was given the honor of authority and respect to actually *name* God. The privilege of giving God a name had never happened before. Adam had been given the task of naming the animals (Genesis 2:19). But here we see a woman, a slave, an indentured child bearer, the distant matriarch of Muslims today, given honor by God Himself. He allowed her to *know Him* and *name Him*.

> She gave this name to the LORD who spoke to her: "You are the God who sees me," for she said, "I have now seen the One who sees me" (Genesis 16:13).

In Hebrew, the word used here for *gave* is *qārā*, meaning to cry out, call; to name; to proclaim, preach.[10] *Rā'ah*, a Hebrew word for see, means particularly in this verse to ascertain.[11] With these meanings in mind, this sentence in Genesis 16:13 could be paraphrased something like this: *Hagar shouted out the name like a preacher. "You are the God who sees me," for she said, "I have now made sure of the One who has made sure of me."*

Many in the church today have placed their trust in God for salvation. But do we understand that He has made sure of us? Is our identity fully in Him? Women in our neighborhoods, our workplaces, our schools, and our cities have no idea that a woman much like them, part of their own ancient story, gave God that name. They might be struggling through their life circumstances, or not. But Muslim women each have the same heart need you and I do: the need for identity, to make sure of the One who has made sure of us. To be made right in our relationship with God, to be seen by the One who gave us life. To know Him. Christian women have an opportunity to show Muslim women that God sees them.

SEEN

When Jameelah came to our clinic so long ago for help and healing, she knew one thing for sure about God. She knew that God saw her. She had not yet, however, seen Him. Her heart, like her disfigured face, was hidden and covered in disgrace. But underneath was hope that because God saw her, help might come.

God offers more than help to us in our shame. He offers hope and a future and, to make us brave, He goes with us Himself on the healing journey. As I closed my hand around Jameelah's that morning in my office, we started a journey together toward the God who sees women everywhere. I showed her the way to the spring called *Beer Lahai Roi,* the Well of the Living One Who Sees Me. (This is what Hagar's spring came to be known as after her encounter with God that day. See Genesis 16:14.[12]) One day I hope we will rejoice together at another spring, called the River of Life.

> Then the angel showed me the river of the water of life, as clear as crystal, flowing from the throne of God and of the Lamb down the middle of the great street of the city. On each side of the river stood the tree of life, bearing twelve crops of fruit, yielding its fruit every month. And the leaves of the tree are for the healing of the nations. No longer will there be any curse (Revelation 22:1-3).

One day we will worship in heaven beside people from every worldview. Together, we will see for ourselves the spring that flows from the throne of God and gives eternal life and healing to the world. Shame will no longer mar the nations, for the curse will be no more.

✤ FOR FURTHER STUDY ✤

1. Read Isaiah 49:14-15. What strong promise does God make here?

2. Continue reading in verse 16. We are not forgotten by God. He sees past the walls men and women build to protect their hearts from pain, disgrace, rejection, from being seen.

3. Read Psalm 139:7-12. What do we learn from this passage about hiding from God?

4. Perhaps you are hiding from God today. He sees you and He is calling you. Let His light come into your darkness and help you. What are the walls that separate you from Him? List them below and write a prayer asking Him to give you courage and help to tear them down.

12

Instead of Broken, Healed

He was pierced for our transgressions, he was crushed
for our iniquities; the punishment that brought us
peace was on him, and by his wounds we are healed.

ISAIAH 53:5

Our footsteps echoed sharply off the walled passageways that wound through the old city like an intricate maze. We were headed to an early morning church service, to a nondescript apartment where we gathered each week to worship quietly, away from the peering eyes of informants and the secret police. My oldest son held his father's hand, leading the way for me and his two younger siblings. Not many people were out at this early hour. The winding streets were deserted and silent but for an occasional cat that darted across the cobbles to the cries of the cart-man plying his fresh mint for the morning tea.

As we rounded a corner, we almost tripped over a person sitting in the dust, half-shadowed by an overhanging doorway. "May God help me through you," she rasped, holding out her hand for alms. Wrapped in a blanket, the woman looked up at us hopefully, her two legs barely visible against the rough stones of the street. They ended abruptly right at the knees.

"Some small offering?" she asked again.

We fished in our pockets for a few coins and looked around, wishing the food shops were open so we could buy bread.

A cranking sound behind us signaled a small store opening its garage-like door. An old man in an embroidered *kufi*, the brimless, round cap worn by Muslim men, busily filled a glass case with fresh, hot baguettes. Standing on tiptoe, our son handed over the coins needed for three loaves as the woman in the dust patiently waited.

She was an amputee. Cultural mores constrained us from openly asking about her story of shame and how she ended up here at our feet begging for alms in a deserted alleyway. The distance between our circumstances and hers loomed between us like an uncrossable chasm. This morning, however, our lives touched between outstretched hands and the common human experience of freshly baked bread.

"May God give you goodness." She smiled gratefully through hearty bites.

"And may God make it easier for you," we rejoined with the customary Arabic blessing.

Saying goodbye, we continued on our way.

"Why didn't we ask Jesus to give her what she really needs?" our six-year-old asked, his question reverberating through the bright morning air and lodging in our hearts.

"What does she really need?" asked my husband.

"New legs. And a house. That's what she needs," he said, his face serious as his eyes probed his father's for affirmation.

As my husband and son quietly discussed the problem of brokenness all around us, I walked the rest of the way in silence, absorbed in my own thoughts about what exactly healing looks like and what the human heart really needs.

SPIRITUALLY BROKEN

Brokenness is a pervasive human problem. It vaunts in vulgar display among the poor and diseased, the disabled and discarded of the nations. It hides deceptively behind the wealthy and comfortable, the powerful and beautiful. Brokenness lurks in every life at some time or another.

To our young child, the woman on the street had two obvious needs: new legs and a roof over her head. Our son's unabashed faith in Jesus's ability to provide for those needs was not unreasonable.

Scripture brims with examples of Jesus's healing of the broken. We are instructed to be openhanded toward the poor and needy, to help them (Deuteronomy 15:11; Mark 14:7).

But to what end is brokenness if it does not lead us to realize our severed relationship with God? *This* is the primary brokenness that concerns humanity. *This* is the most critical issue across cultures and peoples of the world. This need for healing is the one to which all other needs we address must lead. If our doing, our service, and our giving does not lead to the healing of one's relationship with God, then we are offering incomplete restoration to a suffering world.

Complete restoration is impossible apart from Christ. The Healer described in Isaiah 61 peers directly into the souls of women and men and offers hope instead of despair, freedom instead of captivity, justice instead of oppression, beauty instead of ashes, joy instead of mourning, and praise instead of despair. His primary concern, it would appear, is healing for the soul and spirit of each person, not merely the physical condition.

In the 1953 movie *The Robe*, Roman centurion Marcellus Gallio is commanded to crucify Jesus of Nazareth. Afterward, he is tormented by guilt and embarks on a passionate retracing of Jesus's footsteps so that he might examine for himself the claims of the "King of the Jews." This journey takes him to the small village of Cana. That night, as he settles in his tent, the air begins to resonate with the most exquisite harp music and singing he has ever heard. Drawn through the shadowy village into a clearing, Gallio discovers a beautiful young woman sitting on a woven mat, playing the harp and singing the story of the resurrection morning. As Gallio enters, she looks directly into his eyes and sings the final refrain describing the empty tomb. From the centurion's startled expression, it appears this is the first he has heard of Jesus's resurrection after His death on the cross.

Gallio asks the village leader to tell him more about the intriguing singer. The leader explains that her name is Miriam and that, when she was 15, she was struck down with paralysis. Miriam became bitter and angry, poisoning all her relationships. One day there was a wedding and the whole village, except Miriam, went to join the celebration.

Instead, Miriam stayed home and wept over the bitter knowledge that because of her physical disability, she would never have her own wedding day. When Miriam's parents returned home, though, they found her smiling and singing, completely transformed. While the villagers were at the wedding, Jesus had visited with Miriam and healed her broken heart.

This story enrages Gallio, who demands to know why, if Jesus was a miracle worker, He did not heal her? The old, wise leader quietly replies that Jesus had. Gallio was confounded and silenced by the answer.

As the centurion is leaving the next morning, Miriam calls out to him from where she is sitting in a garden near the village square. Confronting his disquiet and confusion, the crippled woman describes with shining eyes the way Jesus healed her bitterness, her disappointment, and her shame. Her fractured heart was made whole, and she was given honor and new purpose. With haunting beauty, she exhorts Gallio to look beyond the physical to the spiritual healing essential to life.

Gallio was baffled by the peace and joy he saw in Miriam, the woman whose paralysis Jesus did not cure but whose heart was made completely new. Healing did not look logical to this Roman tribune visiting the small village of Cana, yet he could not deny the profound power of love he saw in its residents.

God does not always heal like we think He should. Sometimes physical healing does not come. New legs do not sprout for the amputee. The newborn baby does not always continue to breathe. The critically ill do not always rally. These are all physical examples, and perhaps that is our obstacle. Like Gallio, we are angry that God does not act according to our logic and heal the lame, the sick, and the dying. We do not have eyes to see that there is a deeper healing needed, a healing of the spirit within us.

WHAT IS REALLY NEEDED

In His time on earth, Jesus physically healed the lame, the sick, and the dying. But upon closer examination, we discover that His healing of the physical was enveloped in concern for the soul of the one He healed. He saw *completely* every person He met; He saw them mentally, spiritually, physically, and emotionally. With precise wisdom and knowledge of everything hidden, Jesus addressed their needs.

I have learned in my own life to yield to God's greater knowledge of the hidden. Many times, torn and tossed by difficult circumstances and overwhelming challenges, I have knelt and poured out to the Lord what I saw as my primary need. In His gentleness and wisdom, He has shone His light upon a deeper need of which I was not even aware. The raging storm in me calms, the peace of God covers me with comfort, and the next thing is clear. God is a revealing God, and He sees us *completely*.

He completely sees each Muslim woman and knows her greatest need. Her greatest need might not be your friendship or coats for her children. If she does not know Jesus Christ, she is spiritually, critically ill. A healed relationship with God through His Son, Jesus, will bring healing and wholeness to other areas of her life, but the heart is where healing begins. We must cultivate the habit of continually asking Him to reveal what is really needed. His healing might not seem logical or reasonable to us, but we can trust Him with all our needs, both seen and unseen.

UNDAUNTED HOPE

One day as crowds pressed around Jesus, a woman in desperate need of healing worked up the courage to touch the edge of His robe. She was seeking healing for what she saw as her primary need, what anyone who knew her would agree was her primary healing need. But when she touched the God who saw her completely, she received much more than she ever dared hope. The woman's name is unknown, but her story of healing speaks across the ages and will never be forgotten. Her story is found in Luke 8.

> As Jesus was on his way, the crowds almost crushed him. And a woman was there who had been subject to bleeding for twelve years, but no one could heal her. She came up behind him and touched the edge of his cloak, and immediately her bleeding stopped. "Who touched me?" Jesus asked. When they all denied it, Peter said, "Master, the

people are crowding and pressing against you." But Jesus said, "Someone touched me; I know that power has gone out from me." Then the woman, seeing that she could not go unnoticed, came trembling and fell at his feet. In the presence of all the people, she told why she had touched him and how she had been instantly healed. Then he said to her, "Daughter, your faith has healed you. Go in peace" (verses 42-48).

Twelve years is a long time to bleed. According to Levitical law, the woman's blood would have made her ceremonially unclean. This was a type of *positional shame*, alienating her from her family and community. We have previously discussed that, in honor-shame cultures both today and in the time of this Luke 8 encounter, shame was not merely a feeling; it was a position outside one's group. This understanding aids our comprehension of the extent of this woman's suffering. We can deduce that she had been socially restricted or separated for 12 long years. Her loneliness must have been profound, her misery accentuated by the fact that she lived in a collectivist society where one's identity was tied directly to one's relationship with the group. She had broken relationships and a broken identity.

No one could heal her. The story of this woman is also found in Matthew 9:18-26 and Mark 5:22-43. Mark tells us that "she had suffered a great deal under the care of many doctors and had spent all she had, yet instead of getting better she grew worse" (verse 26). Reading the text through the framework of an honor-shame culture, we can assume she was an outcast and had no money. Her situation could not have been bleaker. She had been stripped of all that gave one a position of honor in the society of the time: family, community, health, and money. To many of the onlookers ready to condemn her that day, she was a nobody. It was this nobody, devoid of stature, who had the courage to enter the throngs where she was prohibited and risk the little she had left to touch the garment of the Healer everyone was talking about.

Shame makes us feel like nobodies. We feel invisible, as though no one sees us. We pass through the crowds, obscure and unnoticed, suffering. But even a shamed heart can hold the small, bright flame of hope. Hope is what the suffering woman sheltered deep inside even after all she had endured.

At times in our lives we encounter a soul so shrouded in brokenness that it seems the flame of hope has been stifled permanently. At such times we must run to the God who sees what is hidden, the one who *completely* sees our cloistered soul, and cry out to Him to give that wounded heart courage to reach out and touch His robe.

This woman had courage, and her story offers courage to every woman living with the private brokenness of shame today. She reached out and touched Jesus. The Greek word *haptō*, used here for touch, refers to the kind of touch that is more than mere contact, the sort that creates "some kind of influence or effect...between the two subjects."[1] It is distinguished from the simpler Greek word for touch, *psēlaphaō*, which is a surface touch.[2] Many in the crowd that day pressed in for a look at the Messiah; many were simply touching the surface of Him. They jostled around Him, stepping on His robe, rudely hustling around Him trying to get a closer look. But that one touch, that one effecting, influencing, expectant touch, was distinctly different, and Jesus knew immediately. That touch expected something more from Him. The woman's touch called out like a cry for mercy and reached the depths of God's heart of love for His broken children. His response was immediate and public. "Who touched (*haptō*) me?" He exclaimed in Luke 8:45.

Dumbfounded by Jesus's question, Peter unnecessarily pointed out to the Lord that the people and the crowds were *all* pressing and crowding Him. Peter's implication was, "How can we know who touched You? *Everyone* is touching You."

We can be one of the crowds, curiously pressing on Jesus, the surface of Him, or we can be the nobody who takes the excruciating risk to reach out past our shame and *touch* Him because we cannot bear to remain as we are any longer. We can be assured that all who touch Him expectantly, seeking influence and an effect upon their lives, will reach the heart of God. And we will be changed.

"Someone touched me; I know that power has gone out from me" (Luke 8:46). Some have supposed that Jesus's question and following statement in verses 45 and 46 indicate that He did not know who touched Him, that He was ignorant of the person. I would like to suggest that Jesus knew exactly who she was and was trying to shield her from shame. His mind was set on restoring her honor that day, and He understood *completely* her utter brokenness—mentally, physically, emotionally, and spiritually. From our view today, having heard the complete gospel narrative, we know that the One who stopped her blood that day would one day soon after hang upon a cross to eradicate all our shame, His blood flowing for every woman and man. Through the flowing of the Savior's blood, He would give His life and three days later conquer death forever by rising from the dead. The Messiah walking among the pressing crowds that day knew very well who the "someone" was who had touched Him. He was about to restore her and give her a new name.

HEALED AND RENAMED

Dirty. Outsider. Rejected. Impostor. Bad. Not Enough. The Savior knows every name you believe about yourself. He weeps every time shame pins a new badge on you and whispers its lies into your soul, convincing you the lie is truth. As you bow lower and lower under the burden of shame's condemnation, Jesus's arms stretch wide on the cross, His mighty voice splitting the earth, declaring that Hope is on its way. Life has conquered death. You were meant to *live.*

The suffering woman bowed low into the dusty, rocky road and trembled at Jesus's feet. So many eyes were on her now, gawking at the filthy, outcast woman who dared touch the Teacher. But one set of eyes looked upon her with love and understanding. And to her astonishment, that One called her by the name she most wanted to hear. "*Daughter*, your faith has healed you. Go in peace" (Luke 8:48, emphasis added).

Daughter. We do not know all the details of this woman's family life. But we don't need to. In that single address, Jesus revealed to her and to us the exact center of her pain. He confronted not only the physical pain of a bodily bleeding disorder but also tenderly exposed the emotional, mental, and spiritual pain of rejection and the loss of her relational position as a child of a loving parent. Due to the chronic severity of her condition, she had probably been expelled from worship and forced out of fellowship with her parents. Jesus's loving name for her discloses a deep desire to be loved and cherished, a desire surely unfulfilled in her present state of illness. Can you see how intimately the Savior knew her? Can you hear the intimacy in His voice, the knowledge of her most secret shame, her most private longing? The discovery that we are so personally known and understood by God is what convinces our wounded hearts that we can heal. To be known and loved by the Savior is to be set free from disgrace. Calling her "daughter" was a restoration of this woman's identity. She was restored to relationship with her heavenly Father that day. All other healing flowed from this essential, fundamental reinstatement.

And so it is with us and with our Muslim friends. All healing flows from that one most basic, fundamental restoration. When we are restored to relationship with our Father, we know who we truly are. We are His children, and we are loved. We are set free from shame. Instead of remaining broken, we are healed.

❧ FOR FURTHER STUDY ❧

1. Do you believe shame's names for you? Write them below, then next to them, write their opposites. For example, the opposite of *dirty* is *clean*.

2. Using a concordance in the back of your Bible or an online Bible study tool such as BibleGateway.com, look up the word *clean*. Ask God to speak to you through His Word from the verses containing *clean* and select one verse that describes a truth you want to believe is true about you. For example, Psalm 51:10 says, "Create in me a clean heart, O God, and put a new and right spirit within me" (NRSV). From this verse one might pray, "Lord, help me believe that You have the power to give me a clean heart and a new, right spirit. I am not destined to always feel dirty and embittered inside. With Your help I can be made new." Write your selected verse on a piece of paper and place it somewhere you can see it and memorize it. Using this method, replace the lies with truth, one by one.

3. Have you experienced the most fundamental need for healing, the need for a healed relationship with God? If you have not, you can become a follower of Jesus right now. Pray the following prayer alone or with a trusted friend:

> Dear God, my relationship with You is broken. Shame has separated me from You, and I am a sinner. I believe that You sent Your Son, Jesus, to remove my shame and forgive my sin. I believe that He died for my sin and shame and that You raised Him to life again. I want to trust Jesus as my Savior and follow Him as my Lord. Help me exchange lies for truth. In Jesus's name, Amen.

Instead of Abandoned, Treasured

You will no longer be called, "Abandoned"...Indeed,
you will be called "My Delight is in Her"...For the LORD
will take delight in you...As a bridegroom rejoices
over a bride, so your God will rejoice over you.

ISAIAH 62:4-5 NET

Ratna hummed to herself as she washed the dishes. The kitchen was small and sparse, but it was bright with sunshine today and it was hers. Recently married to a kind, gentle man, Ratna was the mistress of her own home. Her heart swelled with joy as she daydreamed about a little baby boy with dark curly hair like his daddy's.

Crack! The glass she was scrubbing slipped out of her soapy hands, glancing off the edge of the sink and jolting Ratna out of her reverie. Jagged shards sank beneath the bubbles out of sight. In alarm, she drained the water, carefully picking up the pieces and placing them on the counter. The happiness she had felt only moments before dissipated, replaced by creeping dread and fear. Taking a deep breath, she made herself stand taller and squared her shoulders bravely. She would have to face the consequences. Slowly drying the broken fragments, she put them aside and waited for her husband to come home.

A short while later, Lutfi inserted the key into the heavy lock on his apartment door. It always stuck and needed a shove just up to the right to make it open, but he barely noticed anymore. Removing his shoes, he tucked on house slippers, calling out to his wife. Their daily lunch at home together was one of the things he loved about being newlyweds.

But today, instead of her cheery welcome, he found Ratna sitting quietly at the table, a small pile of something sitting cautiously in front of her. Avoiding eye contact, she kept her head bowed down low. *Is she cowering from me?* he wondered.

"Dear one, what is wrong?" he asked.

She slowly looked up, and he could see she had been crying. Her eyes shone with a mixture of fear and courage. Pushing the pile across the table toward him, she replied, "Here. You can beat me now. Please do it quickly."

In Ratna and Lutfi's Muslim culture, the Qur'anic edict[1] placing men in charge of women was widely interpreted to give a husband the right to strike his wife if she displeased him. A particular superstition regarding broken glass urged men to beat their wives to cleanse the house of demonic influence. As a child, Ratna had witnessed her father beating her mother many times.

Now she sat immobilized, waiting for the generational pattern to repeat itself in her marriage. Lutfi stared at the broken shards of glass, carefully displayed on a soft towel, then looked at his young wife. She was beautiful, her brown eyes flecked with gold. Her hair lay softly against her flawless skin, the graceful outline of her face lovely to him. She sat stock-still, bracing herself for the customary punishment.

Lutfi placed his hands gently beneath her chin, lifting her face to his. "We know a better way now. We do not live by the old law any longer. We live by the law of love. Jesus the Messiah has taught us how to love one another. Do not be afraid. You are my treasure."

Ratna leaned toward her husband, relief and wonder filling her heart. Jesus had taught them a better way. She was cherished, by her God and by her husband. What God was this who, instead of abandoning women, treasured them?

Ratna and Lutfi's story is true. My husband and I were privileged to hear it retold the next Sunday evening as the couple came for the church meeting in our house. Lutfi looked away, a shy smile on his face, and allowed Ratna the full pleasure of relating to us the astounding tale. She bubbled over with joy, and Lutfi seemed to grow a little taller as she spoke.

The two had been married for less than three months. Their wedding had been an occasion for exceptional joy, for they were the first Christian couple in our small church of Muslim converts to be married. The tiny congregation of fewer than 20 members had celebrated for three full days, feasting and singing, dancing and praising God. Eyes sparkled with bright hope for a new generation of Christian families among the predominantly Muslim population of their homeland. Ratna and Lufti were leading the way to the New Way, the way of love between the Savior and His followers and between husbands and wives.

Transformed marriages in any culture are one of the most convincing proofs of the redemptive power of Jesus Christ. Marriage, in its origin, was intended to be a picture of God's great love for us. The love between husband and wife has the potential to reveal the deep and mysterious passion God has for His treasure, you and me. Tragically, in so many broken systems of humanity, marriage has fallen far from this ideal. But there is hope, for God is bent on rescuing the abandoned. It is the passion of His great heart, and there is no fear, no despair powerful enough to stop Him from rescuing us.

THE FEAR

Many women in the Muslim world today live in fear of abandonment. Abandonment comes in different forms. Widowhood leaves many women without means to support themselves. Shame and its resulting expulsion from the family or tribe leaves women alone as outsiders. Destruction and war rob Muslim women of their loved ones, leaving them destitute and frantic, in addition to being racked with grief.

Fear of abandonment is a common female experience. It can be observed in women around the globe. In parts of the world where women enjoy equal rights and access to education, this fear can sometimes be observed in the rigor with which women work to create a place for themselves in their societies. Armed with education, stature, and strength, they become their own rescuers, pursuing independence as insurance against abandonment. In cultures where women struggle under the burdens of illiteracy, injustice, and unfair legal systems, the fear of abandonment relegates women to manipulation of the system, desperate acts of self-sacrifice, and the pursuit of power over fear through supernatural means.

For a Muslim woman from an honor-shame worldview, where belonging to one's group is paramount to self-dignity and identity, abandonment can be an expected consequence if she breaks the group's rules. Many Muslim women in the world today live resigned to the reality that they must strive to earn their position of belonging. Even then, it is not guaranteed to last. They become industrious, willing to do anything to override the limitations set upon them. I have seen women in remote Muslim villages walk for days to find a special kind of food to please their husbands and keep them faithful. I have watched Muslim mothers severely scold their daughters for the misbehavior of younger brothers, knowing these little girls must be raised to follow the rules and bear honor for the next generation. If they don't, they may be rejected, cast outside the group, or disgraced. *Abandonment*, it turns out, is just one more word for shame.

A woman will do anything to survive, even risk her life to protect her family. We see a gripping example of the extremes to which she will go in the story of a woman named Rahab.

THE PROMISE

Scholars argue whether Rahab of Joshua 2 was a prostitute or an innkeeper at the time of the invasion of Jericho. In any case, her dwelling became center stage for one of God's most startling rescues of a woman and her family. Her entire existence and that of her family was shifting, on the verge of complete and utter change. Did she know it? Did Rahab have a clinching feeling in the pit of her stomach when she opened the door to those burly Israelite spies sent by their commander to look over the city? How did she know what she must do?

Rahab was surely unaware that, as one outside the tribe of the Lord Most High, she had been set apart, devoted, marked for divine service unto the one true God. But that is exactly what happened to her.

During a raid in which God commanded His people to devote the city of Jericho and all that was in it to the Lord, destroying every living thing within its walls, Rahab was both spared and set apart for divine service (Joshua 6:17). The Hebrew word *herem* translated in this verse as "devote" meant to destroy totally *or* to devote. It denoted something either devoted unto divine service or marked for destruction.[2] In Arabic, the similar word *haram*, also a derivative of the triliteral Semitic root H-R-M, is still used to mean something forbidden or sacred. Rahab was *herem*, set apart, marked by God, for divine service. Her destruction had been forbidden by God before the two spies ever struck a deal with her. Rahab was marked for divine service that would extend far beyond her actions during the fall of Jericho. Her story gives glorious insight into the words of 1 Corinthians 2:9: "'What no eye has seen, what no ear has heard, and what no human mind has conceived'—the things God has prepared for those who love him." Rahab chose the Lord, the God in heaven above and on the earth (Joshua 2:11, from her declaration of faith). She had no idea then what a beautiful story God had planned for her life.

Rahab would become an ancestor of the Messiah Himself, one of only five women listed in His genealogy as recorded by Matthew (1:5). But as she stood on the threshold of her house in the ancient wall, staring up at those strong warriors, she had no idea she was so treasured. Her only thought was how to avoid abandonment and death.

Like many women from an honor-shame worldview, she was willing to do whatever it took to preserve her family. She saw her opportunity for rescue and seized it, offering the Canaanites' enemies refuge and help. Her initial motives might not seem pure to a Western reader. They appear selfish, driven by fear and a desperate desire that she and her family survive pending destruction. Her concern was not for the glory of the God of Israel and the fulfillment of His promises to His chosen people. Rather, her thoughts were about herself and the people important to her. But no matter her starting point, Rahab was designated to reveal God's glory and honor. God drew her to Himself out of her concern for her loved ones.

Rahab's progression of knowledge is important to note. Much is said about what she *knew*. She began in Joshua 2:9 by telling her guests that she *knew* they had the favor and power of the Lord on their side. She and her people were terrified of the Israelites. She then detailed what she *knew* of the mighty deeds of their God. Their bold deeds and the extraordinary acts of their powerful God were interwoven as she described all she had seen and heard. Rahab *knew* she and all of Canaan were terrified of these men. She *knew* they carried the greatest power on earth, all because of the favor of their God. All of this knowledge had been revealed to Rahab by the customary human means of report and observation.

This knowledge had a fascinating effect on Rahab's own faith. Human knowledge had led to divine, God-given knowledge in her. In Joshua 2:11, she disclosed her own belief that the God of Israel was the one true God: "For the Lord your God is God in heaven above and on the earth below." Sometime during this terrifying ordeal, Rahab had taken a quiet step from unbeliever to believer in Elohim.

This is so often the pattern I have seen with Muslim women. They watch and observe; they listen and think deeply. They examine the gospel message and secretly wonder if it could be true. If they are brave, they ask questions and read the Bible. Then one day, quietly and with little fanfare, they make that life-changing step to belief in the saving power of the Rescuer, Jesus Christ. Their human knowledge and understanding are engulfed by the spiritual revelation that Jesus Christ is the Savior. They are convinced, and the honor burden transfers from their shoulders to the Messiah's. "Our lives for your lives!" the men assured Rahab in response to her request to be rescued (Joshua 2:14). "Jesus's life for your life!" we are assured in response to our cry to be delivered from shame and sin. "This is how we know what love is: Jesus Christ laid down his life for us" (1 John 3:16).

Rahab believed the warriors' promise, it resulted in her being included in the line of her ultimate Savior. She later became the wife of Salmon (a prince of Judah in the line of David), the mother of Boaz, and one of the ancestors of Christ (Matthew 1:5). The scarlet cord she tied in her window to identify her house in the chaos of the coming invasion was a picture of the scarlet sacrifice her descendant Jesus would one day make to identify His followers as *rescued, not abandoned*.

Rahab's faith was so significant that later, when Joshua, the commander of the Israelite army, finally shouted his declaration of war, he included her preservation in his instructions (Joshua 6:17). As he sent troops thundering forth in an adrenaline rush of built-up anticipation and certain victory, he reminded them of the covenant made to preserve Rahab and her household.

The battle for God's promises in our lives is thunderous and real, making His enemies tremble. But in the midst of the war, He remembers His covenant, He preserves His treasured ones, and He never leaves them abandoned in the tumult.

❦ FOR FURTHER STUDY ❧

1. Luke 18:27 says, "Jesus replied, 'What is impossible with man is possible with God.'" If you carry shame, it may seem impossible to ever believe you are treasured. Write Luke 18:27 on paper, put it where you will see it regularly, and memorize it. Ask God to change what you believe about yourself and to replace the lie that He has abandoned you with the truth that you are His treasure and He takes delight in you.

2. Read the following verses, and from each one write down what is true about those who place their faith in God. Ask God to help you believe what He says is true about you.

   - Isaiah 41:9-10
   - Isaiah 49:15-16
   - Joel 2:25-26
   - John 8:31-32

14

Instead of Uncertainty, Security

My sheep listen to my voice; I know them, and they
follow me. I give them eternal life, and they shall never
perish; no one will snatch them out of my hand.

JOHN 10:27-28

The sun had set and it was time for *salat-al-maghrib*.[1] The prayer rugs had been carefully laid out to face Mecca, the Islamic city that is revered and honored as the holiest city in the religion of Islam and the central place of prayer for Muslims. Seven-year-old Areefa stood quietly beside her mother, listening for instructions. Today she would officially begin praying *salat*. She had dressed carefully, making sure only her face, hands, and feet were visible.[2] "Stand up straight and make sure your feet are close together, pointed toward the *qiblah*,[3] my daughter," her mother reminded, demonstrating on her own mat. "Now, let's make our intention."

I am going to pray salat, thought Areefa to herself, just as she had been taught.

Her mother lifted her hands to either side of her chest, then crossed them, her right hand over her left. Areefa imitated her slowly and carefully. In Arabic, Areefa's mother began the familiar chant, "God is the greatest." For several more minutes, she quietly intoned the prescribed prayers and positioned her body accordingly. Areefa joined in easily, having watched and listened to this special time of prayer since she was a small girl. After the final prayer, Areefa and her mother looked at each other. Her mother's face was beaming.

"Well done, my daughter! You are a faithful girl."

Areefa smiled back shyly. She was a compliant, obedient child and always respected her parents. As Areefa grew older, she became adept at praying *salat*. One day when she was nine years old, after performing the required prayers, she asked her mother a question that had been burning in her mind for weeks.[4] "Mother, why must we pray in Arabic, and not our own language?" It made no sense to Areefa that God required her to pray in a language she did not understand. Didn't He create all languages? Perhaps it was shameful to even question Him.

Her mother looked up from the rice she was sorting, her face clouding with annoyance, and answered, "My daughter, this is how it has always been done. Do not ask questions." Areefa was dissatisfied with her mother's dismissal and silently determined to search until she found an answer that made sense. Areefa was a truth seeker. Her intellectual hunger was growing, and the questions inside her heart were also increasing. They would not go away even if she tried to ignore them.

Areefa had sensed God pursuing her since she was a small child. Deep down inside, she believed He didn't object to her inquisitive mind. She felt compelled to search for Him and find out everything possible about Him. She wanted to talk to God about all the details of her life, not only perform prescribed prayers at prescribed times every day in a language not her own. Surely God the Most Kind and the Most Merciful would not rebuke her for wanting to know Him as personally as possible.

Is He angry with me? she wondered. Areefa's mother constantly chastised her about the way she dressed, the way she played, the way she served tea. Her father always seemed to be concerned that she did not embarrass him by breaking the rules girls were supposed to live by. Was God like that? Areefa felt in her heart that He couldn't be. Looking to her parents for guidance, she grew more confused.

Areefa's father verbally assailed his daughters and wife regularly, calling them foul names and accusing them of shaming him. At the same time, Areefa began to notice that he would flirt with other women in front of her mother, telling women how beautiful they were and making lewd, admiring comments about their bodies. Eventually it became clear to Areefa that he was having affairs. During all of this, Areefa's mother remained silent. Areefa watched the imbalance in her parents' relationship with growing dismay. How could her mother allow this to continue? Again, her thoughts turned to God. Surely her father's behavior was wrong in God's sight.

As she grew into a young woman, Areefa's insecurity and confusion increased. All the rules she had learned about how to be righteous and how to gain God's favor seemed unstable and uncertain. They clearly were not working for her mother. Her mother followed all the rules carefully, yet she was not valued by her husband. Her life was miserable. As Areefa thought about it more, she concluded that her father's contradictory behavior must be against Islam. God surely could not approve.

She turned deeper into Islam, determined to find the true source of security for women. At age 19, she was accepted into a prestigious European University for Muslim students. She had a passion to learn about Islam and then teach it in Western societies. Areefa's greatest desire was to honor God and discover truth. Now she would become an Islamic seminary student, fully able to examine it for herself. Her plan was perfect, she thought. In the source texts of her religion, the Qur'an and hadith, she would discover truth that finally made sense. After she found it, she would teach truth to others and make the world a better place for women like her mother.

The Bible says, "Call to me and I will answer you and tell you great and unsearchable things you do not know" (Jeremiah 33:3). Areefa had no idea, but her cry to know the truth about God had been heard, and even then He was guiding her to Himself. The way would be a surprising one, a path she never could have expected. Areefa *would* find the truth, and she *would* teach it to others, making the world a better place for women like her mother. Since the first day when, as a tiny girl, Areefa began to desire a relationship with God, He was running toward her, overcoming every obstacle, every rough place, every crooked path to get to the one He loved. Areefa had no idea how near she was to the truth for which she longed.

A faithful student, she pursued knowledge with zeal, devouring everything her professors at the university could give her. But as she examined the life of her beloved prophet of Islam in the Qur'an and hadith, she was horrified to discover evidence that, instead of refuting the oppression and misuse of women, he actually supported it. The prophet's sexual life particularly disturbed Areefa. His marriage to Aisha took place when Aisha was six years old and was consummated shortly after her first menstruation at age nine.[5] Later, the leader of Islam took his adopted son's wife away from him.[6] Areefa's love for her prophet filled her with anguish as she discovered these passages. She had never been taught this. Rather, the prophet had been venerated as the example for all Muslims to follow. Well, she thought cynically, her father's behavior would have been approved by the prophet.

One day, as she labored through this crisis of faith, she came home to find her roommate texting with one of their married professors. With a guilty look, her roommate grabbed an overnight bag and dashed out the door. A few days later Areefa confronted her. "Were you meeting our instructor?" Eyes sparkling with false hope, her friend replied, "He loves me. And it's not forbidden, because we did *mut'a.*" *Mut'a* is a temporary contract of marriage for the purpose of sexual pleasure.[7] Islam had made a way for the pleasure of men to override their marital obligation to their wife.

Areefa was flabbergasted. This same professor was one of the most admired and respected teachers of Islam in her university. She and her roommate had frequently stayed up late at night dreaming of their futures as college professors in the United States, dispelling the wrong impressions of Islam as a religion that devalued women and placed the burden of men's sexual impropriety upon them. But as her mind swirled, only one thing was clear to Areefa that night: Islam was no refuge for women.

The next morning she arranged a meeting with a male professor she trusted. She would present her findings in the Qur'an and hadith to him and ask him to help her understand. She had carefully compiled them in preparation for her dissertation on the topic of possible negative preconceptions in Muslim thought about female sexuality. She continued to uncover evidence that seemed to support a clear suppression of women's sexuality and value in Islam. Areefa was hanging on to a thread of hope she was wrong about her religion and her prophet.

The instructor looked at her title, and his face shadowed with grave concern. Glancing at her before quickly flipping through the texts she had cited, his eyes flashed a warning. *You are on shaky ground here,* they seemed to say.

Maybe I am just nervous, Areefa thought as she waited for his response. She was growing anxious and uncomfortable, the opposite of what she had expected to feel in the presence of this wise man's counsel. "This topic is unacceptable," he said seriously. "You are casting doubt upon our holy sources, and this cannot be done by one who is seeking to one day propagate our honorable religion to others." Areefa sat immobilized, unable to breathe. "You must choose a different topic for your dissertation," he concluded. With that, he rose to his feet from the ornate, red leather chair behind his dark cherry desk.

Areefa found her breath and felt a flash of courage surge through her. "But, sir, as a woman, I can offer a perspective men cannot. Please, help me understand these confusing texts."

"I have already given you my answer. You have until Friday to give me your new topic. If you choose not to, you may return home for a few weeks and reconsider how important your degree is to you."

With that, he walked to the door and opened it, gesturing for her to depart. Areefa stood in disbelief and walked slowly out, taking her unanswered questions with her. Two weeks later, Areefa was on a plane headed back to her childhood home, to the place it all began. She had refused to abandon the subject of her dissertation. She would never abandon her pursuit of truth and its impact on women.

Over the months that followed, she began to explore other religions and what they said about women. After reading a biographical book written by a former Muslim thinker who had become a follower of Christ, she began to read the Bible. What she found there astounded her. She was shocked to learn that Jesus showed compassion and love for women, even for prostitutes.

Jesus loves me even though I am a woman? Jesus sees me as an equal to any man? More questions flooded Areefa's heart and mind as she examined the life of the Messiah. Ravenous for answers, she read the Bible day and night, examining the Scriptures deeply. Jesus taught that everyone deserved to be loved, regardless of their sin and shame. He knew they needed love, not condemnation. This deeply impacted Areefa. The dirtiness and unworthiness she had carried for years began to slip away with each word she read. *I am God's daughter!* she thought to herself, overwhelmed. She could feel His great understanding of women's suffering. For the first time in her life, Areefa felt loved by God instead of condemned. The insecurity she had carried all her life was replaced with stability and certainty that was guaranteed to last. Jesus had said it Himself: No one could take her out of His hand. Strong and brave, Areefa could finally rest in the knowledge that she was safe and secure.

SEEKING SECURITY

Strength does not guarantee security. Throughout history, strong women have faced adversity, persevered, worked hard, searched high and low, and in the end found that God was the ultimate, unshakable source of stability in their lives. Ruth was one such woman. We spent time in chapter 7 examining her tenacious journey to the threshing floor, where she sought the protection of a kinsman redeemer named Boaz. Ruth was intimately acquainted with suffering, death, and abandonment. Her spirit was immovable, and with unflinching courage, she faced her circumstances and marched right into the center of God's story of rescue for humanity. In fact, she played a starring role in your security and mine.

The book of Ruth opens with the dramatic narrative of how an old woman named Naomi and her young daughter-in-law, Ruth, came to find themselves clinging to each other for survival. All of the men in the family, Naomi's husband and his two married sons, had died, leaving the women without home or protection, in the present or the future. In Naomi's mind, the solution was easy for her daughters-in-law. They were young and still had a chance at stability if they remarried. She implored each of them to return to their mother's home, declaring,

"May the Lord enable each of you to find security in the home of a new husband!" (Ruth 1:9 NET).

Grief had blinded Naomi to any hope for her own future. Left all alone and wracked with despair, she concluded that God's hand was against her. Despite their resistance, she urged her daughters-in-law to leave her. "At this they wept aloud again. Then Orpah kissed her mother-in-law goodbye, but Ruth clung to her" (Ruth 1:14).

The Hebrew phrase meaning "clung to" is used seven more times in the Old Testament, and every one of those times it is used in reference to holding fast to God.[8] The Israelites were exhorted repeatedly to hold fast to the Lord as their one security and identity. Deuteronomy states it beautifully: "Listen to his voice, and hold fast to him. For the Lord is your life" (30:20). How intriguing that the writer of Ruth, traditionally believed to be that great God-clinger Samuel, would use this poignant and meaningful phrase to describe Ruth's dependence upon Naomi.[9] If Samuel was indeed the author of the book of Ruth, then it is no surprise he knew commitment when he saw it. Samuel's life was a direct result of his mother Hannah's habit of holding fast to God (1 Samuel 1).

Ruth's security was firmly in her mother-in-law, and she was committed. Resourceful and overcoming, Ruth refused to give up, let go, or shut down. We do not know many details of Ruth and Naomi's relationship before this pivotal moment, but the evidence of the younger woman's deep love for and dependence upon Naomi is clear as she clings to her, refusing to find security elsewhere.

Ruth was an outsider. She was a Moabite, while Naomi's family was from the tribe of Judah. Ruth had not grown up worshipping the merciful and loving God of Abraham, Isaac, and Jacob. Her god was Chemosh, the god of the Moabites, a terrifying fish god who demanded human sacrifices (2 Kings 23:13).[10] Worshippers wouldn't cling to a god like this for security. Ruth must have watched the faith and practice of her husband's family with fascination. "Stop urging me to abandon you!" Ruth responded to Naomi's insistence she leave.

For wherever you go, I will go. Wherever you live, I will live. Your people will become my people, and your God

will become my God. Wherever you die, I will die—and
there I will be buried. May the LORD punish me severely if
I do not keep my promise! Only death will be able to separate me from you! (Ruth 1:16-17 NET).

With that, the matter was settled. Ruth had clung to Naomi and
cemented her commitment with a declaration of faith in the God of
Israel. Maybe the thought of leaving Naomi triggered the realization
for Ruth that she would also be leaving the comfort of Naomi's faith.
It was time to make a decision, and Ruth chose faith in the God whose
strength and character she had come to understand through Naomi.
Reliance upon Naomi had grown into reliance upon Naomi's God.
Naomi's faith was now her own.

Ruth and Naomi turned their faces toward the future and headed
together down the road to Bethlehem, the tiny place where one day the
longed-for Messiah would be born. But they were not thinking of that
at the moment. They did not know how important Bethlehem would
eventually be to all of humankind. No, those two strong women were
fixated upon their own salvation and posterity, their survival together
without husbands or sons.

It was the beginning of the barley harvest when they arrived in
Bethlehem, and the fields were buzzing with activity. Servants worked
from sunrise to sunset collecting the harvest. Levitical law instructed
the Israelites to leave margins of their fields unharvested, as well as to
leave behind any produce that fell to the ground (Leviticus 19:9). This
was a way to allow the poor and those who were foreigners living in the
land to come along after the hired harvesters and collect provision from
the fields. Landowners oversaw this process carefully, deciding how
wide each field's margin would be and therefore how generous they
would be to those in need. This practice of working the fields behind
the laborers was called gleaning.

Ruth understood hard work, making it on her own. As both a
widow and a resident foreigner, Ruth was fully qualified to be a gleaner.
After seeking permission from Naomi to collect grain in this way, Ruth
went out to the fields to work. It just so happened she began in a field

belonging to one of Naomi's relatives, a man described in the Hebrew of Ruth 2:1 as a fortress, a safe place, mighty, strong, valiant, a man of substance and wealth.[11] His name was Boaz, and he was a compassionate man who practiced careful oversight of all he owned. When he saw Ruth, he immediately asked his foreman about her. After hearing that she was Naomi's daughter-in-law and a diligent worker, he quickly established her position in the group, saying, "Listen carefully, my dear! Do not leave to gather grain in another field. You need not go beyond the limits of this field. You may go along beside my female workers" (verse 8 NET). She was no longer a gleaner but a harvester, with all the protection Boaz's authority afforded.

Ruth was used to being an outsider. She was not accustomed to being shown favor and honor. Reminding him of her lesser value, she declared, "Why have I found such favor in your eyes that you notice me—a foreigner?" (verse 10). Those who know the shame of being outsiders are skeptical when they encounter honor. Some feel the necessity to remind others who they really are: less than. They have believed the lie so long that it has become their identity. Honor and value seem too good to be true. Ruth reminded Boaz of who she believed herself to be. What Ruth did not realize was that Boaz already knew everything about her, even her faith in the Lord, the God of Israel, under whose wings she had come to take refuge (verse 12). Boaz is a Christ-figure in this Old Testament story, foreshadowing for us the character of the Messiah who would one day come through his family line.

Like Ruth, we are skeptical when we encounter honor. Can it be trusted? What about my secret shame? Honor and value can seem too good to be true. Some of us have believed for so long that we are not important, that we are tarnished, dirty, or spoiled, that we think this is who we will always be. What we do not realize is that Jesus already knows everything about us, even the tiny firefly of hope that darts around in our dark thoughts on our most desperate days. He has already drawn the lines on the field of our freedom, and we have been given a position of honor, security, and protection in His name.

Ruth's encounter with Boaz that day was only the beginning of her security story. Theirs was the kind of love story that blows apart the tight seams of bondage that hold hearts in the grip of shame and insecurity. As we learned in chapter 7, it turned out that Boaz was what the Bible calls a kinsman redeemer, one who was obligated to carry on a dead relative's name by purchasing his land and marrying his widow. Boaz not only gave Ruth a position of security in his harvest field, he married her. Three generations later, Ruth and Boaz's great-grandson David would slay a giant and become king. One day Ruth would be known as one of the ancestors of Jesus Christ, Savior of the world, guarantor of security for all women and men.

FOR FURTHER STUDY

1. Read Deuteronomy 32:3-4. Describe the progression of praise in Moses's song. What names does Moses give God? What does each one signify?

2. Read 2 Samuel 22:1-4. What do Moses's and David's songs of praise have in common? Write your own song of praise to God.

3. What comfort do these verses offer the shamed?

Part Three

Honor
Shared

15

Stubbing My Toe Against Sin

This righteousness is given though faith in Jesus Christ
to all who believe. There is no difference between Jew
and Gentile, for all have sinned and fall short of the
glory of God, and all are justified freely by his grace
through the redemption that came by Christ Jesus.

ROMANS 3:22-24

"We are all sinners. Our sin separates us from God," I earnestly explained to my friend Haifa. Her baby girl cooed softly as if she agreed, looking up at me with innocent, beautiful brown eyes. The infant's cleft lip was barely visible and would be simple to repair. We only had to work a bit to get her hemoglobin levels up enough for her to have surgery.

Haifa's friends had sent her to my door after seeing me on television at a recent cleft lip and palate project in the local hospital. The need that brought her to me originally had been eclipsed by something else I had to offer: a safe place to ask her private questions about God. I was a *Masihia*, or Christian. Haifa was hungry to know what I believed, and her questions challenged me.

"Don't worry about your sin," she interrupted me. "You are a good person and God is pleased with you. You help children. You pray and give God praise. You even fast!"

Confused, I paused mid-sentence. I was launching into the four spiritual laws I had always shared with those who were seeking God.[1] Haifa was lost and I was found. I was making it clear to her how to be saved. Didn't she realize her problem? I was giving her the answer! Frustration rose in me as I concluded that Haifa was not really listening. She had *missed the point*.

Islam told her that if she observed religious rules like prayer, fasting, and giving to the poor, she would gain favor with God. If she was compassionate and served those less fortunate than her, she surely would see her good deeds outweigh the bad, the scales tipping in her favor before Him. And if she was very, very good, she might gain entrance to heaven one day. But who knows? God had the final say, and He might change His mind. As for me, in her mind, I was fine. If anyone was secure in her position of favor with God, it was me. It was obvious, wasn't it? Any person who had left her parents, her home, and her culture to help provide children with free surgery was surely tipping heavily on God's good side. I even did some of the same things Muslims did, like praying and fasting. Heaven was probably a foregone conclusion for a *tabiba*,[2] or doctor, as everyone believed me to be. I was practically Muslim, according to Haifa's view. In fact, she often said, "You are much like a Muslim. You are getting close."

"No, you don't understand, my friend," I continued. "It doesn't matter how much good any of us do, we can never make ourselves sinless. We can't be good enough on our own to stand before a holy God."

"God will forgive *you*. You are a good person. Don't be anxious, my dear," she replied, patting my leg reassuringly. She thought I was worried about *my* salvation! Who was comforting whom and with what truth here? It was clear to me that I was the one *missing the point*.

My Western gospel appeal, founded on the paradigm of sin and forgiveness, was stubbing its toe right up against one of the most stubborn, foundational beliefs in Islam: work hard and you might be good enough to get into heaven. When I explained to Haifa that sin was the reason we were separated from God, she already had a solution, prescribed by her own beliefs. Do good works to solve the problem.

Many Muslims, when they encounter sincere followers of Christ, are initially surprised and confused to discover that Christ followers do many of the same things Islam holds in high regard. Faith, fasting, praying, and charity are four of the five pillars of Islam. The fifth is pilgrimage to the holy city of Mecca. Through her Islamic framework, Haifa interpreted my religious acts as signs that I was a person of true faith and perhaps even close to becoming a Muslim. The problem with my explanation of the gospel was that it did not seem relevant to any need Haifa felt she had. Islam resolves the sin problem with the option of doing good. Sin is rendered benign if you do it in secret without bringing shame to your group. And there are always good works if you need some extra equity against its effects in your life.

The approach I was using resulted in my defense of my own badness. The truth I most wanted her to understand was that Jesus is God's provision for man's sin and it is only through Him we can have a personal relationship with God. Instead, I found myself in the awkward position of convincing her that even a "good" person of faith like me was too bad to appear before God. Haifa refused to believe me. Her own worldview had persuaded her otherwise.

THE WESTERN WORLDVIEW: SINNERS IN NEED OF A SAVIOR

The truth is, we have all sinned and fall short of the glory of God (Romans 3:23). When sin entered the world through mankind, humanity fell away from the unblemished honor and glory it once shared with God. Ever since, sin has held people like a tether, keeping them from reaching the glory of God on their own. The rope is too short, too tight, and leads to death instead of life. No matter our culture or worldview, we are separated from God because of sin.

The sin-forgiveness approach to the gospel is a valid one. We stand in need of forgiveness, a righteousness apart from the law. No amount of our doing good or obeying the law can make us right again. We need a Savior. Therefore, God has given us a way to righteousness through faith in His Son, Jesus. This is the gospel of Jesus Christ.

Two-thirds of the world today see everything through the lenses of honor and shame, not innocence and guilt. Through the honor-shame worldview, much sin can be overlooked as long as a person follows the rules of the group. My family experienced this firsthand living in the Arab world throughout the terms of three different American presidents. Americans are keenly interested in the private lives of their presidents and are often offended by their behavior and personal choices. It is wrong to commit adultery. It is right to give to charity. It is wrong to spend campaign money on personal comfort. It is right to meet with factory workers and listen to their concerns. Americans are pretty clearcut in our idea of what is right and wrong. We judge our leaders and form our opinions of them accordingly.

In contrast, our Muslim neighbors were unconcerned about the personal lives of American presidents, often excusing behaviors that incensed Americans. Instead, through the honor-shame worldview, leaders who were friendly and diplomatic with the Muslim world were admired no matter what their personal moral choices. Abiding by the rules of the group covered any personal infractions and even made the leader more endearing.

Approaching the gospel by appealing to one's sin burden and need for forgiveness can sound like unnecessary nonsense to a listener from an honor-shame worldview. Although those holding to this view would agree man's separation from God because of sin is true, it might not be understood as an impossible problem needing God's provision to resolve. Those from an honor-shame worldview need to know how the gospel addresses shame. How we begin our gospel discussion with the majority world could make a big difference in how the message of salvation is understood.

❧ FOR FURTHER STUDY ❧

1. Read Jeremiah 3:25 and answer the following questions.

   - In this passage, Israel laments both her shame and her sin before God. What is Israel's response here to shame?

   - Describe a time when shame made you want to hide.

   - How does hiding from God affect our ability to obey Him?

   - In your own words, describe how shame keeps us from confronting our sin or the sin of others.

2. How did Jesus Christ resolve both sin and shame?

16

The Trumpet Blast of Honor

"At that time I will deal with all who oppressed you.
I will rescue the lame; I will gather the exiles.
I will give them praise and honor in every land
where they have suffered shame. At that time I will gather
you; at that time I will bring you home. I will give you honor
and praise among all the peoples of the earth when I restore
your fortunes before your very eyes," says the LORD.

ZEPHANIAH 3:19-20

For 20 years, I worked with people with disfigurements, people with mobility impairments, and those whose natural beauty was distorted by forces beyond their control. Now I have laid aside my scrubs and surgical caps for a pen and paper, and I work with those who have been disfigured by the lies of shame. With these instruments, moved by the hand of God's Spirit, my prayer is that the gospel that offers forgiveness from sin, righteousness I cannot earn, will also offer honor in the place of shame for all who have been maimed by its dark power.

Jesus is the healer of the shamed, be they men or women. My friend tells the story of how he learned the honor gospel through the life of his disabled son. Born with cerebral palsy, his son James was a living declaration of the shame-removing gospel in their Arab community. In that culture the arrival of a firstborn son was cause for great celebration, exalting the father to a place of honor. The father would typically become known from that day on by his firstborn son's name. That son would grow into manhood, in turn carrying his father's name forward to the next generation, perpetuating the family honor. In the sad and unexpected event that a son was born with a disability, the restraints of disgrace would prevent that father from taking his firstborn's name, waiting instead for the birth of a second, unblemished son.

As a follower of Christ, however, my friend did not ascribe to that practice. From the beginning, he was known to all as Abu-James, the father of James. He rejoiced over his son and believed God had created him with value and purpose. Neighbors and all who met the family were fascinated to see that James had not brought shame upon his father. James and his family challenged the belief that a disability relegated one to a position of shame. It was clear to everyone that God honored, not rejected, James. That honor and value flowed into the lives of the community, changing it at the core. Hearts were opened and the message of Christ's love was demonstrated to a people who understood the problem of shame and its power to separate one from others and from God. My friend believes his son's impairment is God's manifest glory in the midst of his Arab community, declaring to a people devastated by shame that the Messiah removes disgrace and bestows honor instead.

OUR NAMES, AND HIS

Like James's father, our Father in heaven bears His children's names with love and compassion.

> Can a mother forget the baby at her breast and have no compassion on the child she has borne? Though she may forget, I will not forget you! See, I have engraved you on the palms of my hands; your walls are ever before me (Isaiah 49:15-16).

God will not forget us, no matter how high the walls shame has built around our hearts.

One ancient Jewish custom involved tattooing one's hands or arms with paintings of Jerusalem or the temple, creating a constant reminder for the bearer.[1] The imagery in Isaiah 49 is not only a reminder of God's love for Israel. It is also a promise to all who come to God through faith in Christ: *I will not forget you.* Later, the Messiah's wounds from the nails in His palms would become yet one more poignant illustration of God's constant remembrance of us. His thoughts are toward us.

God's name belongs to His children. He bears our names with tender remembrance and we bear His. This is a glimpse of the beautiful reciprocity, the giving and receiving, of value and honor that is integral to a healthy and loving relationship between God and people. Regardless of their station, physical form, weaknesses or strengths, or genders, all who believe in Jesus Christ have the right to be called children of God. With that noble right gained by faith, they are given honor and value, hope and a future. Relationship with God is restored, and they are no longer separated from Him.

God is a gatherer of His people. He longs to gather His children, to comfort them, to relieve their heavy burdens, and to heal their broken hearts. Through it all, He reveals His own honor and glory. The Bible overflows with beautiful imagery of God gathering those who have been scattered by sin and shame. Those once lost are found; those once rejected are accepted. For those from an honor-shame worldview, the image of God as a gatherer is particularly significant. Shame casts them outside. To be brought inside again is the essence of salvation.

For some women from honor-shame cultures, Muslim and non-Muslim alike, the shame they experience is a result of someone else's sin against them. One of the most horrific modern examples of this is the thousands of Yazidi women taken from their villages in northern Iraq and made *sabaya*, or sex slaves, by the Islamic State (ISIS). One woman who escaped from bondage reported that, as she was carried away to the slave market, she begged God to forgive her.[2] Shame does that to its victims. Shame makes its victims believe their expulsion is their fault. They believe they are inherently bad, and the responsibility of the true perpetrators is covered by this cunning lie.

The good news of the gospel for any woman victimized by another's sin is that God has sent a rescuer, Jesus Christ, to remove her shame and defend her honor. He is a God of deliverance and a God of justice.

She is loved and cherished by God. She has great value in His sight. He gathers her to Himself, to the refuge and safety of relationship with Him.

The honor gospel, as I called it in this chapter's title, is not a new and different gospel. Rather, it is one dimension of the liberating good news for all peoples of the earth. For some, the power of sin has immobilized them, and the message of forgiveness is the door through which they run to the arms of God. For others paralyzed by shame, the message of honor is the trumpet blast, signaling victory and homecoming. The gospel of Jesus Christ is multifaceted, for our God is a multifaceted, dynamic God. He meets every need of every person. Depending on our worldview, the starting point can make all the difference in understanding His great salvation.

 **FOR FURTHER STUDY**

1. Read Zephaniah 3:19-20 and list everything God promises to do for those who trust Him.

2. Among these promises, is there one or more you long to see in your own life? Write it below.

17

The Hidden Room

There I will give her back her vineyards,
and will make the Valley of Achor a door of hope.

HOSEA 2:15

THE NATURE OF SHAME

The room was dank and musty, a tiled space beneath the family salon. You wouldn't know it was there if someone didn't show you. The present occupants lived in the house for many months before they discovered the door. Drab and hidden among the mosaic wall of the spacious and sunny courtyard, it concealed narrow stairs leading down to these sparse living quarters. The room had a feeling about it. It felt like terror.

The new owners asked around, seeking information about the purpose of the hidden room. Their questions were usually met with dismissal, or a *tsk-tsk* with wagging finger, warning them that the story was not a good one. But one day an old neighbor told the tale over a cup of hot tea. In a voice barely above a whisper, she explained that a young girl had lived in the room, brought from her country tribe in the far mountains. She had been sold to the wealthy urban family to be a servant, where her task was to serve the men of the household for their pleasure. In return, she was given the hidden room, food, and clothing.

The old lady leaned close and whispered, "I saw her one morning. She wore the night on her face. They took God's light from her eyes." In Arabic, there are two words for light: *daw'*, or man-made light, and *nour*, the light of God. This young servant girl was removed from her family and tribe and made a slave. She was covered in shame. The light of God was shrouded in darkness. Shame had concealed her core identity.

The first lie spoken to the first woman in the Garden of Eden was dripping with shame. The lie stripped woman of her position as honored and valued in relationship to her Creator. Shame, not animal skins, was Eve's first covering on that fateful day. The nature of shame is that it conceals what is true and good.

Since that pivotal moment in the history of mankind, a thief has crept through the generations, robbing souls of their most important asset, their value. The worth of humankind lies in the truth that we were created in the very image of God. Every woman and every man bear upon their souls the imprint of God Himself, His own reflection. Here is the birthplace of honor, the value of the human soul. Shame hides this intrinsic truth from those it harms.

With shame came the taking of value and, consequently, the veiling of true identity. The robbery of humankind's identity is at the center of shame's work. Humanity has been in desperate pursuit of identity every moment since. Their intended, created identity as people valued and loved by God has been obscured by shame.

Shame is a lie. Shame tells the bearer that she must hide. Shame persuades its listener that she is not important and never will be. It shouts that no matter how hard one works, worships, prays, and does right, one will never be *enough*. Shame levels the accusation that you are too broken, too damaged, or inherently bad. You are *outside the camp*. Go and hide yourself.

As we have learned, honor and shame are actual positions in society for those from the honor-shame worldview. Language reflects this positionality. In Arabic, the new title *Hajj* (for men) or *Haja* (for women) is earned when one has made the *hajj*, or sacred pilgrimage, to Mecca. In Pashto, the position of honor is described by the word *ghairat*. Sayed Naqibullah, Afghan author and linguist, explains on his cultural blog: "In Afghan culture, to tell someone that he/she does not have Ghairat is considered one of the biggest insults. If one doesn't have Ghairat in

Afghan society one will not be considered honorable; and if he/she is not honorable in this society, he/she could be alienated by most of the members and life can become very hard."[1] Words for one in a position of shame are unmentionable and frequently used as curse words.

One's honor or shame is directly dependent upon one's position in the group, be it a family, a tribe, or a nation. In the beginning of time God created one group, one family, one tribe, and one nation. Man and woman belonged with God, and their position was secure.

The shame carried by millions today has its origin in the beginning, when the deceiver proposed independence from God. A position outside the group. A "better" position. A more powerful one. In believing this lie, Adam and Eve lost, rather than gained, a better position. Separation from God led to separation from their true worth. Shame engulfed them and changed the course of their lives.

For those shrinking into the shadows of shame, identity is at the core of the crisis. The nature of shame has not changed. The deception it breathes continues in this era. Shame paralyzes its prey and makes her believe she is of no worth. The light of God, intended to shine in her, grows dim with despair. But there is hope. There is a power greater than deception, a power that overcomes the lie of shame. That power is love. The Creator, driven by blinding love, pursues the one He has created, offering her honor in the place of shame. She can belong again, safe and secure in her position of value, knowing for certain that she is loved. She can come out of hiding.

HIDING AT NOON

Anyone who has lived in the dry, arid parts of the world where water must be drawn from a village well understands that water is collected early in the morning before the heat grows to uncomfortable temperatures. Women and children rise with the sun and make their way to the well, jars and buckets balanced carefully on their heads or hips. The daily water collection is like a morning newscast, where all the events of the village are reported and discussed. For those in an honor-shame culture, this time of fellowship is a foundational part of community building and social bonding.

In the book of John, chapter 4, we find a woman who has come to the village well at the sixth hour. Time was counted from sunrise, making the sixth hour around noon. The woman was alone, laboring to fetch the day's necessary water at a time no one would gladly choose. No one ventured to the well at high noon except those who were avoiding their neighbors or who had been rejected from the group and pushed into hiding.

This particular woman was an outsider among outsiders. Her people, the Samaritans, claimed to worship the same God as the Jews, but disputed with them about the location of the chosen place they must worship. Samaritans believed it was Mount Gerizim, while Jews believed it was Mount Zion in Jerusalem. This conflict caused much division between Samaritans and Jews. Leaders from both groups taught that it was wrong to have any contact with one another.

As the woman made her way to the well alone, Jesus made His way up the winding road to Galilee. The road took Him right through the country of Samaria, nestled alongside the valley called Achor, or "trouble," which was named after the calamity Achan's sin brought upon all of Israel after the battle of Jericho (Joshua 7:1-26). Referring to God's promised redemption of His people, the Old Testament prophet Hosea beautifully referred to the Valley of Achor as a doorway of hope (Hosea 2:15). The hope's promise was closer than anyone could have imagined that day in the town of Sychar, in the country of Samaria, where a disgraced woman did the mundane daily work of going to the well for water.

The Samaritan woman lived a troubled life. She was about to meet the Doorway of Hope Himself, sitting quietly and wearily beside her village well. The Valley of Achor would indeed transform into a doorway of hope for her on this ordinary day of hiding in plain sight.

Jesus made His way to the woman's village and sat down at the well. He could have stopped somewhere else to rest and refresh Himself. But He did not, and I imagine this was because she was on His mind. I wonder if perhaps her emergence from the hiding place of shame was a priority in His heart that day. She mattered to the Savior. Perhaps He arranged His day to set her free.

Jesus did not avoid her. The Savior does not avoid our shame as we do. Instead, He quietly draws near and waits for us to open up about our darkest secret. There is no pressure, only His presence patiently waiting and loving us, knowing us better than we know ourselves, drawing us out of our shells. He is not constrained by time. He will wait as long as it takes.

Are you hiding? Do you believe Jesus intentionally pursues you? He might already be sitting on the wayside of your mundane task, waiting for you to lay aside your heavy vessels of burden and talk awhile. He is waiting with love, and He knows you better than you know yourself. Jesus is no harsh and abrasive confronter of our secrets. He is a gentle Savior, and your freedom is on His mind today. Shame hides from you what is most true about you: that you are loved by God and you matter. Draw near to the story of the woman at the well and learn what shame hides. It might surprise you.

LOVE

> When a Samaritan woman came to draw water, Jesus said
> to her, "Will you give me a drink?" he asked (John 4:7).

The irony! The Water of Life asked a woman, a Samaritan, for a drink! She was an outsider, in every way positionally dishonorable to Jesus the Jewish Rabbi. She was startled by His brazen request and reminded Him of her position. "You are a Jew and I am a Samaritan woman. How can you ask me for a drink?" (verse 9).

How often when approached by the Savior do the shamed try to convince Him they are unworthy! The false beliefs they hold about themselves are so deeply embedded that even when love draws near they cannot believe it is meant for them. The Samaritan woman thought there must have been some mistake, that somehow the thirsty man who sat at her ancestors' well had not heard how things were for Samaritans and women.

There was a time in my relationship with my husband, long before we were engaged, that I perceived his feelings for me were becoming more serious. One night as the snow fell all around us, we sat bundled in blankets under an ancient tree, sipping hot chocolate. I decided it was time for me to tell him about the trauma of my past and disclose how damaged I truly was. He deserved to know the truth about me, I thought, so that he could walk away before it was too late.

I will never forget the tangible quietness that came over him as he listened intently. When we parted that night, I was sure he would decide to stop seeing me. Shame had convinced me that I was worthy of abandonment. To my astonishment, he did not leave me, and we were married the following year. We will soon celebrate 25 years of marriage. When love draws near, shame insists we are unworthy. It is a cruel lie, hiding the truth that we were, in fact, *made to be loved.*

TRUTH

> Jesus answered her, "If you knew the gift of God and who it is that asks you for a drink, you would have asked him and he would have given you living water." "Sir," the woman said, "you have nothing to draw with and the well is deep. Where can you get this living water? Are you greater than our father Jacob, who gave us the well and drank from it himself, as did also his sons and his livestock?" Jesus answered, "Everyone who drinks this water will be thirsty again, but whoever drinks the water I give them will never thirst. Indeed, the water I give them will become in them a spring of water welling up to eternal life." The woman said to him, "Sir, give me this water so that I won't get thirsty and have to keep coming here to draw water" (John 4:10-15).

Shame hid the truth from this woman. She was unable to think beyond the concrete words Jesus said to her. Their wisdom was lost on her. She knew all about water and the drawing of water. She understood that one needed empty vessels to draw deep from the well, to fill and to carry back home for the day's work. She also knew that it was a necessary daily task. The one hidden in shame knows the daily toil of her burden. She was too tired to perceive anything beyond the physical and practical. Living was laborious. Anything to make it easier was welcome. Wasn't this man offering a quick fix, a magical solution to her daily labor? Listening with physical ears and looking with physical eyes, this was the only conclusion she could draw from His curious words.

Her lack of spiritual understanding did not deter Jesus. He was patient, because He had her freedom in mind. His next command would change her life. Well-placed and smack-dab in the middle of her ordinary day, it was the key that would unlock the door to all her secrets. "Go, call your husband and come back" (verse 16). Probing deeper, He began to reveal that He knew all about her. He knew her shameful past, the wrong decisions she had made, the reasons she had come slinking to the well at a time no respectable woman ever would. It is then, when shame in all its slippery darkness was confronted, that the woman's understanding made a dramatic shift. Light slipped into the conversation like a wedge intent on breaking through.

The truth was rising, no longer hidden. It had begun its crescendo, conducted by God Himself, and no one could stop it.

PURPOSE

That Jesus met the shamed woman exactly where she was is highly significant. He did not stand far off, send a messenger with special instructions for how she was to approach Him, and wait to see if she would show up. He intentionally came directly to her, right where she labored.

Jesus met the Samaritan woman geographically in her village of Sychar. He met her physically at a well, at the place where the common human experience of thirst is typically quenched. Jesus met her intellectually on her level of understanding, and from there He drew her higher. He met her where she was spiritually, affirmed what she already knew of salvation, and challenged her to learn more. He met her emotionally in her hiding place, exposing the secrets she was working hard at noon to cover.

Jesus comes to us exactly where we are and as we are. He meets each of us, all the way. We do not have to go to a special place to find Him. He is near us even now, waiting for us to notice, to engage, and to be courageous enough to talk to Him.

As the Samaritan woman bravely conversed with this stranger, she began to perceive that He was no mere man. His words shone with wisdom and truth no man could conjure.

> The woman said, "I know that Messiah" (called Christ) "is coming. When he comes, he will explain everything to us." Then Jesus declared, "I, the one speaking to you—I am he" (John 4:25-26).

In that instant, the woman was transformed from hider to proclaimer. The one who purposefully planned her day's work away from the prying eyes of her neighbors found her purpose. She didn't hide. Rather, she shouted to all who would listen, "I think I have found the Messiah!" The crowds grew and, before she knew it, they all followed her back to Jesus. She was not only in the group again, she was leading it. Her purpose was no longer hidden by shame.

The Bible records, "Many of the Samaritans from that town believed in him because of the woman's testimony," and "He told me everything I ever did!" (verse 39). What kind of Savior is this, who knows our secrets and loves us anyway? Shame cannot hide in the presence of the Savior. What has been carefully concealed is uncovered and what is secret becomes known. The result is healing and liberty.

As He approached Sychar that day, Jesus's eyes were certainly set upon the freedom of one disgraced woman. But He also knew that her freedom would lead to the freedom of many others. This is the glorious way of Christ, the way of the one who gives honor instead of shame.

FOR FURTHER STUDY

1. Read Luke 7:36-50 and answer the following questions:

   • What kind of woman came into the Pharisee's house? What was her reputation in town?

   • Where did she stand after she entered the house?

   • What did she do for Jesus, even as she stood in a position of shame and insecurity behind Him?

   • What was the response of the religious men to this woman?

   • In verse 44, Jesus turned toward the woman and addressed the men. In that moment, He changed her position with Himself. She was no longer behind Him, but face-to-face with Him. Then, looking at her, He addressed a man. What is the question He asked Simon?

   • How does Jesus's physical change in position illustrate the woman's spiritual change in position with Christ?

2. In what position do you stand with Jesus? Has shame forced you into hiding, afraid to face Jesus, but bravely longing to meet Him?

18

The Guarantee

For there is one God and one intermediary
between God and humanity, Christ Jesus, himself
human, who gave himself as a ransom for all,
revealing God's purpose at his appointed time.

1 TIMOTHY 2:5-6 NET

Isana met me at the door and quickly ushered me inside, pulling me through the pulsating crowds of men in the small front room of her family's apartment. Her face was shining with unwiped tears, and she had exchanged her typical, trendy European fashions for a dark *abaya* and headscarf. Her father had died. Nothing else really mattered that day. Now was the time for wailing and intercession. Would the prophet help her father reach heaven? The men chanted and shouted, their Arabic supplications punctuated with pleading phrases on behalf of Isana's father. They implored their mediator, the prophet of Islam, to bring the dead man safely into the presence of God.

Out of respect for my friend, my own hair was concealed by a scarf, my *abaya* covering everything except my hands and face. Isana led me into a second room in which all four walls were lined with couches covered in rich green and gold brocade. Women filled every seat, their sorrowful eyes peering curiously at me as I entered. The atmosphere in this room was starkly different. There was no shouting, no prayer. The air seemed to quiver with a mixture of fear, grief, and uncertainty. Whereas the men charged the gates of heaven like warriors on horseback, confident in their supplications, the women sat quiet, somber, anxious. Perhaps they were praying silently in the privacy of their own minds. I know I was. *God, let them know the only mediator between God and humanity, the man Jesus Christ, who has made their position in heaven sure,* I prayed.

THE GOSPEL OF CHRIST

The women in attendance that day were not only physically separated from the men by a wall but were also assigned to a different room. More importantly, they were spiritually separated from God by the belief that, even at the end of life, there is no guarantee they will be granted entrance to heaven. For my Muslim friends sitting in that room, solemn and downcast, hope for heaven lay in their ability to follow the rules. If they could do enough good deeds to outweigh the bad, they might be accepted by God on that final Judgment Day.

For followers of Jesus, hope lies in the grace of the Messiah Jesus. Because no one can stand blameless before a holy God, Jesus stands for us. The sinless, holy Savior has taken our place, making it possible for us to be reconciled to God. Through Christ, our place in heaven is guaranteed.

For Muslim or Christian, eternal separation from God is the ultimate loss of position, the ultimate disgrace. Without certainty of salvation, there is no resolution for shame or sin. No list of rules followed, no good behavior, no carefully observed religious practice can accomplish the holiness required to belong to the family of God. Salvation was accomplished one way, through one person, God incarnate, the man Jesus Christ. This is what honor reveals.

THE LOVE OF GOD

John 3:16 says, "For God so loved the world that he gave his one and only Son, that whoever believes in him shall not perish but have eternal life." Love is the beginning of honor's revelation. God loves you and me. For Western ears, this famous phrase from John 3 has become cheap, splashed on bumper stickers and billboards with bright yellow smiley faces, to be passed over and dismissed. But for the one who has spent her life trying to be righteous, striving like young Areefa in chapter 14 to follow religious rules dictating even how she holds her wrist when she approaches God in prayer, the message "God loves you" is nothing short of radical. Many Muslim and non-Muslim women alike conclude God is far away from their daily struggles.

One eloquent, university-educated Muslim woman I know spends her time poring over the names of God, examining how one might experience God's love personally. I have witnessed hope and joy illuminating the faces of Muslim women in both villages and cities as they considered for the first time that God might love them personally. At the heart of humanity is a desire to be loved. Muslim women are no different.

Islam is not without its concept of a loving God. One of His ninety-nine Islamic names is *Al-Wadud*, the Loving, the Kind One.[1] The Arabic word *wudd* means "love, affection."[2] Non-native Arabic speakers may be more familiar with the word *hubb*, which also means "love and affection."[3] In Muslim tradition and experience, *wudd* is love demonstrated by action, and *hubb* is love itself. According to Islam, God gave Himself the name *Al-Wadud*, the One who demonstrates His love by giving.[4]

The gospel of Christ underlines this belief with striking clarity: God indeed demonstrates His love for us by giving. He loves us so much that He gave His very life to restore us to loving relationship with Him. Our honor and value, distorted and misplaced when sin marred our friendship with God, were secured forever by this ultimate gift of sacrifice.

Al-Wadud of Islam requires service and works to gain His love, as demonstrated by the hadith writer Bukhari in Book 1, Hadith 386: "My slave keeps on coming closer to Me through performing Nawafil [voluntary prayers or doing extra deeds besides what is obligatory] *until I love him...*"[5] The same hadith goes on to describe an exquisitely beautiful love relationship between God and his slave, although such love is possible only after that condition of effort and labor on the slave's part is met.

The words "until I love him" haunt me. So many women, Muslim and non-Muslim, are trapped in the place of "until." Working for approval, striving for acceptance, they cherish a hope that one day they will be valued with a love so loyal, so fierce, that it can never be shaken. This desperate longing drives them to exhaustion, depression, sadness, perfectionism, and a plethora of other symptoms of the heart that does not know its value to God. The good news of the gospel is that there is no "until I love her" with Jesus Christ. He demonstrated His love for us when He laid down His life to secure ours for eternity.

The God of the Bible has already accomplished the labor, the effort, the death required to redeem us. There is no human endeavor worthy or capable of accomplishing the salvation of a human soul. As the psalmist writes, "No one can redeem the life of another or give to God a ransom for them—the ransom for a life is costly, no payment is ever enough" (Psalm 49:7-8). Life is costly. It is valuable, of great worth, a sum only its creator can fully measure and redeem.

We cannot work for God's love. We cannot earn it. *We have it through Jesus Christ.* Any attempt to reach God apart from His provided Mediator is futile. Those who have been harmed by shame's deception struggle greatly to believe this. Even as I write this book, I hear shame's voice mocking me, reminding me of what I used to believe about myself before Jesus's truth set me free. Shame is powerful and loud. It screams its lies, demanding we work faster, try harder. It demands that we strive and strain. Or, if you'd rather, just give up. Quit, exhausted, shrinking back into the shadows of rejection, accepting the lies that you are *bad*.

It bears repeating: Love is the beginning of honor's revelation. With honor comes defense and protection. The honor of Jesus offers security to those who accept His invitation to believe. They are brought into a safe place, a refuge, a sure and certain fortress that cannot be shaken. Men and women alike can know that the honor He gives is neither uncertain nor changing. It is eternal and unshakable. The time for wailing and intercession is past. The Mediator has made a way to heaven, guaranteed.

FOR FURTHER STUDY

1. Biblical honor reveals that we do not have to wait until we are good enough to be loved by God. Read 1 John 4:19. Who loved first, us or God? What is the significance?

2. Read Romans 5:6-8. How did God demonstrate His love for humanity? Describe what we were like when Christ died for us.

19

A Little Light for the Journey Home

I did not see a temple in the city, because the Lord God
Almighty and the Lamb are its temple. The city does
not need the sun or the moon to shine on it, for the
glory of God gives it light, and the Lamb is its lamp. The
nations will walk by its light, and the kings of the earth
will bring their splendor into it. On no day will its gates
ever be shut, for there will be no night there. The glory
and the honor of the nations will be brought into it.

REVELATION 21:22-26

Wool rugs dyed in bright red, blue, yellow, and orange dotted
the rocky riverbank like scattered quilt patches waiting for
a giant to stitch them together. The women had spent the
entire morning beating them, scrubbing them, rinsing them, and dip-
ping them in the flowing stream to rinse away the all-purpose olive oil
soap. These hard workers now gathered in clusters under shady trees,
stewing hot tea over open fires and breaking soft, flat loaves of bread
to share.

Like the laborers on the riverbank, we have beat the rug, scrubbed
it, and rinsed it, so to speak. It is time to lay our subject out to dry and
gather to discuss how to practically apply all we have learned.

The gospel of Jesus Christ removes our shame and bestows honor
instead. This is the central message of this book. I have experienced it

personally and have observed it in the lives of women around the world. It follows that understanding the honor-shame perspective could be an instrumental starting point of sharing the gospel with those harmed by shame, particularly if they are from a culture that holds the honor-shame worldview. The message of value, love, and honor is transformational for anyone who knows the cruel, silencing grip of disgrace and rejection.

A MESSAGE FOR EVERYONE

When I first began writing this book, my passion and purpose was to create a volume that contained tools I wish I had had in my many years living in an honor-shame culture among Muslims. No matter how fluent I became in Arabic, no matter how close my relationships or how immersed my family and I were in the ancient community, I was always aware that I could see only dimly the beautiful people around me. I could understand only in part their practices and perspectives, and was painfully aware of my imperfection as I shared with them the hope and freedom I had found in Christ. I was constantly disappointed in my own ability to understand and clearly express how great the love of Christ was for them in a way they could comprehend. Therefore, the idea of digging deep into themes of honor and shame in the Bible intrigued me and filled me with excitement and hope. Perhaps this was the missing strategy.

I increased my study, my conversations about honor and shame, and my exposure to wise Christians who are discussing the topic today. I began to pour out my heart on the subject at conferences and in publications and workshops. Across the globe, I met people who all were asking to know more about this worldview. The increasing conversation only fueled my passion and validated in my mind the goal of this book.

An American friend challenged me one day. "Can this perspective not also be for the many Western Christians covered in shame?" she questioned. "What about us? This is revelatory. How many Western Christians know they are forgiven, yet carry incredible burdens of hidden shame? And they have no idea how to remove it."

I realized that, in my zeal, I had overlooked my own culture. We all, regardless of our worldview, need *all* of the gospel. We need forgiveness. We need to know we are loved and have value. We need power over fear. We desperately need every single drop of the gospel and all its nuances and mysteries, its power to divide bone from marrow and reveal every last crevice of human weakness. Like blinding sunlight, it chases the darkness away and bleaches our stained souls. For some, that stain is called shame.

Naturally, as Westerners, we have historically read the Bible through our own innocence-guilt worldview. Yet God used people from an honor-shame worldview to write the sacred text, and it was injected into an honor-shame culture. The Bible does not need to be contextualized to be understood by those from that worldview today; our perspective does. As we look for honor-shame themes in the Bible, we will not only become better communicators of the gospel to Muslims, we will grow ourselves in our understanding of the gospel that not only forgives sin but *also* removes our shame and bestows honor instead.

Thus, my own purpose for this book has grown and expanded beyond my original intentions. Isaiah 55:9 reminds us that "as the heavens are higher than the earth, so are my ways higher than your ways and my thoughts than your thoughts." I am so thankful for wise and godly counselors who have stretched my thoughts toward God's and helped me find His higher way. This book is for you, whoever you are. May the Lord reveal His higher thoughts and higher ways for your life through its words.

LIGHT RECEIVED, LIGHT GIVEN

When we lived in the deep bush of East Africa, I was often asked for a little paraffin, also called kerosene, to light my neighbors' small, handmade tin lamps. I made sure to always have a supply of kerosene to give away in addition to what was necessary for my own lantern. I used to love the sight of a friend walking down the pathway from my house, the little light she had received from me flickering like hope in the blackness of the African night. Can you see the light in your mind's eye with me?

Maybe you want to share light with your neighbors and friends. You want them to know there is hope in Jesus Christ. Fill your own lantern first, then the overflow will be a constant supply for those who know you can be counted on for light and truth. If we want to reach Muslims or anyone writhing in the ropes of shame's lies, we must first come to the Savior and let Him deal with our own souls. We must choose to disclose to Him what He already knows about our hidden places, trusting the Savior to heal us. And *He will heal us*. He will show us a love so great it cannot be measured and will never be stolen from us. When we experience that love, that knowledge that we are valued by God Himself, we will not be able to see the end of the line of people at our door wanting a little light from our steadfast supply.

> Come, let us return to the Lord. He has torn us to pieces but he will heal us; he has injured us but he will bind up our wounds. After two days he will revive us; on the third day he will restore us, that we may live in his presence. Let us acknowledge the Lord; let us press on to acknowledge him. As surely as the sun rises, he will appear; he will come to us like the winter rains, like the spring rains that water the earth (Hosea 6:1-3).

Let us acknowledge the Lord. Let us *press on* to acknowledge Him. He chose to shroud His beauty and glory in our shame on the cross. Then, with all the power of heaven, He ripped it off like the discarded grave linens that could not hold Him in the tomb and secured our honor forever. We choose to trust Him, then we keep doing it every day of our lives, bringing as many with us into His presence as we possibly can. The gospel of Jesus Christ removes our shame and gives honor instead.

❧ FOR FURTHER STUDY ❧

1. Read 1 Corinthians 1:26-28 and answer the following questions.

   • In what condition are most people when God calls them to follow Him? In what condition were you?

2. How did God choose to reveal His wisdom to the world?

   • Do you believe that your life can be used by God to rescue others from shame? What steps do you need to take? Write your response.

Keys to Identifying Honor and Shame in Scripture

One of the best ways we can equip ourselves to understand honor and shame in the Bible and in turn share it with those from an honor-shame worldview is to read it for ourselves. This can be hard to do, though, when one has always read Scripture through a different cultural lens. I have developed the questions below to help you read the Bible through the lenses of honor and shame. The stories that follow will guide you through two examples of how to apply these keys.

1. Identify the hidden/covered issue: What does shame *conceal*?

2. Identify how God reveals and restores honor in this passage: What does honor *reveal*?

3. Identify how you can apply this to your own life or when sharing the message of honor with a friend: What is the *appeal*?

Honor and Shame
Key Applications

Read the following Scriptures and apply these keys:

- What does shame conceal?
- What does honor reveal?
- What is my appeal?

LUKE 7:36-50: JESUS IS ANOINTED BY A SINFUL WOMAN

What does shame conceal?

This account of "a sinful woman" illustrates the close relationship between sin and shame. In this passage a woman who had lived a sinful life, one described by the Greek word *hamartōlos* as heinous and habitual, had the courage to enter a Pharisee's house as Jesus dined there.[1] Her sinful choices in life had rendered this woman "sinful" in the eyes of the community, especially the religious leaders. We understand from the honor-shame culture of the time that her sinful choices and consequent disgraceful reputation also socially exiled her, placing her in a position of shame. She had an immoral reputation and had been rejected from society as a result. Her positional shame concealed from Simon, the Pharisee hosting the meal, the woman's potential for redemption and forgiveness. He could not see past her sin and shame.

He was appalled by her actions. Simon's reaction was appropriate within the context of his worldview. But Jesus, as we will see, challenges any worldview that devalues people, rendering them unredeemable.

We have learned that shame makes its bearer feel not only rejected but dirty and unworthy. In the culture of Luke 7, such a woman was also considered spiritually unclean. It is possible that shame also concealed in her heart an anguished hope that spiritual uncleanness did not equal permanent rejection from God Himself. Her tearful sacrifice of that item most precious to her, her costly alabaster jar of perfume, revealed how desperately she hoped for redemption, to be made clean again.

What does honor reveal?

Jesus restored honor by using the woman's sacrifice as an illustration to teach about forgiveness. He also gently rebuked the righteous, "right with God," Simon, pointing out that his love for Jesus was small compared to the "sinful" woman's. She understood clearly that she needed much forgiveness; she understood the value of Jesus's forgiveness and showed Him her faith by loving Him greatly in return. Simon was taking Jesus's forgiveness for granted and forgetting his own great need for forgiveness. To use a woman to teach a man a spiritual truth was shocking and potentially offensive in the male-led culture of that day. The underlying theme of this story is Jesus's restoration of the woman's honor by pointing out her value to God.

What is the appeal?

Women need to know they are valued by God. Nothing they have done has rendered them too unclean to be made clean or forgiven. It is never too late to surrender one's reputation to God. The sinful woman demonstrated courageous faith by going to the feet of Jesus in the presence of her accusers, those who had judged her a ruined person. Forgiveness is available for every person who makes this bold, risky step toward the Savior. But Jesus does not stop at forgiveness. His goal for you and me is complete freedom. Jesus removes our shame and gives honor in its place, for He sees our worth. What we have been hiding, the burden we have carried silently, shamefully, the Savior gently takes from us and declares us forgiven and honored. Our faith has saved us, and we are sent forth in peace.

Refugees and women in transit may not have not been able to do what Muslims normally do to make themselves "clean" before God. They have probably not been able to do ablutions, or ritual cleansing, before prayer. Maybe there has not been an acceptable place to pray. Maybe they have been forced, or have chosen, to commit shameful acts in order to survive. The message of acceptance and cleanness before God through Jesus Christ is a powerful truth for them.

1 SAMUEL 16:1-13: SAMUEL ANOINTS DAVID

What does shame conceal?

In the honor-shame culture of Samuel's time, honor was given to the oldest son. Outward strength and attractiveness made one more likely to gain the approval and esteem of one's group. This is still true today in many societies. In his search for God's chosen king, Samuel was following the cultural dictates of honor and shame. When he saw Jesse's firstborn son, Eliab, he thought he had found the next king. In this passage, human rules of honor and shame hid the truth from the man of God. The truth was disclosed when God said to Samuel in verse 7, "Do not consider his appearance or his height, for I have rejected him. The LORD does not look at the things man looks at. People look at the outward appearance, but the LORD looks at the heart."

This story turns the honor-shame paradigm upside down, from the value placed on birth order to the human tendency to bestow greater honor and esteem based upon one's outward appearance. Shame can conceal from even the wisest among us God's perspective about a person. It can conceal his worth to God, his gifts, and his future purpose. Shame can conceal wise judgment from us.

What does honor reveal?

Samuel, though he was God's servant, still needed God's help to see the true worth God saw in David. The Author of original honor knows what is in our hearts, and He reveals in this passage the source of true worth. Our hearts reveal our faith. David was the youngest and the smallest of his brothers, but his heart was full of faith in God. He was a worshipper and a poet. He hungered to know God. Honor also reveals that no matter how the world measures us outwardly, God measures our hearts. He sees our gifts, our purpose, our future. God sees our worth, and He loves us.

What is the appeal?

It can be either frightening or comforting to know that God sees our hearts. If we are hiding sin and shame, we might shrink back from His examination and hesitate to draw near. If we have been battered by the unfair judgment and rejection of others, the thought that God sees the truth about us might be liberating. No matter what one's response, fear or hope, it is never too late to bring our hearts to the One who can heal them, clean them, and make them strong again. He sees past the scars and scratches to who we were meant to be, and our future stretches out before us, upheld by a God who goes before us and loves us each step of the way.

Acknowledgments

To…

The One who leaves the 99 to take the lost lamb in His arms and bear it to safety, I thank you with all my heart for rescuing me from shame. Thank you, Jesus.

My best friend and teammate in all things, my husband, David. You have encouraged me and supported me every step of this journey. Thank you for believing in me more than I did myself at times and holding the vision of lives set free before me so I would run the race with endurance. You have shown my eyes what the honor and love of Jesus really look like.

My three children. Thank you for sharing your mom with Muslim women around the world and bearing with me when I pounded the keyboard at all hours of the day and night. Thank you for not minding cereal for dinner on deadline weeks, for your hugs at just the right time, and for telling me never to give up. I love you.

Dad K, thank you for speaking a father's blessing on this fatherless girl and showing me what honor looks like. I will always walk on the high road because you and Mom K showed me how. Thank you both for taking me in and making me yours.

My mother, who bravely faced the shame, thank you. Our story is still being written with grace.

Dr. Jarvis, you were the first to tell me I must, not should, write a book. Roland Muller, my mentor and encourager, I could never have done this without you. This book belongs to both of us. Hannah Thompson, my dear lifetime mentor, thank you for endless cups of tea and truth. You helped me heal. Edie Melson, my writing mentor, you have given so generously and patiently to me, and I am indebted to you for helping me become an author.

Jane, who opened the door.

The Bomb Squad, the prayer team behind this book, you know the private battles and victories it took to get this far.

My superior beta readers, Jen, Beth, Kit and the Muller family. You made the book readable and reachable.

Jami Staples. Thank you for becoming my fellow visionary, dreamer, friend, and colleague. I hope this book answers some of your nagging questions.

Fouad Masri, Werner Mischke, Jayson Georges, and Jackson Wu. Thank you for your leadership and guidance, and for the many emails and phone chats for your opinions and counsel.

To Floyd and Blackie's, my favorite coffee shop. Thanks for not charging me rent and for making me the best cup of coffee in three states.

David Van Diest, my literary agent. You have been a rock of wisdom and encouragement. Thank you.

The diligent and dedicated staff at Harvest House Publishers, especially Kathleen Kerr, Jessica Ballestrazze, Kyler Dougherty, and Betty Fletcher.

And finally, the many brave women who inspired this book's message. I will always be grateful to you for demanding to know the God who gives honor instead of shame.

Notes

INTRODUCTION

1. For further insight into Folk Islam, I recommend Dr. Rick Love's book *Muslims, Magic and the Kingdom of God* (Littleton, CO: William Carey Library, 2013).

2. In her dream, Jesus used words directly from Scripture, though she had never read the Bible. Muslims around the world consistently report dreams of Jesus speaking words they later discover are directly from the Bible. In this young woman's case, His words were a quote from John 14:6: "Jesus answered, 'I am the way and the truth and the life. No one comes to the Father except through me.'" The command "Follow me" is repeated numerous times in the New Testament when Jesus invited someone to become His disciple (see Matthew 4:19; 8:22; 9:9; 19:21; Mark 2:14; John 1:43; 21:19).

CHAPTER 1

1. Jon Ronson, "Monica Lewinsky: 'The Shame Sticks to You Like Tar,'" Guardian.com, April, 22, 2016, https://www.theguardian.com/technology/2016/apr/16/monica-lewinsky-shame-sticks-like-tar-jon-ronson.

2. Monica Lewinsky bravely addresses what she calls a "culture of humiliation" in her striking TED talk, "The Price of Shame," https://www.ted.com/talks/monica_lewinsky_the_price_of_shame.

3. This is a true scenario. During an afternoon gathering for tea with Muslim female friends one day, the women discussed the victim's guilt at length, much to my distress and attempted intervention. The verdict among them was firm: it was her fault, and she deserved whatever she got.

4. https://www.etymonline.com/word/shame.

CHAPTER 3

1. https://www.biblegateway.com/resources/matthew-henry/Isa.45.1-Isa.45.1-4.

2. https://www.biblegateway.com/resources/matthew-henry/Isa.45.1-Isa.45.4.

3. *The Cambridge Bible for Schools and Colleges* exegetical commentary, which looks at original biblical languages, describes the use of *surname* in Isaiah 45:4 as bestowing "honorable names" upon Cyrus (Cambridge University Press: 1882–1922), Isaiah 45. *The Pulpit Commentary* explains the surnames given to Cyrus in Isaiah 45 as "designations of honor" (Hendrickson Publishers, Peabody, MA: 1990), Isaiah 45.

4. Jayson Georges and Mark D. Baker, *Ministering in Honor-Shame Cultures* (Downers Grove, IL: IVP Academic, 2016), 17.

5. Malcolm Gladwell, *Outliers* (New York: Hachette Book Group, 2008), 167.

6. Hans Wehr, *The Hans Wehr Dictionary of Modern Written Arabic,* edited by J. M. Cowan (Urbana: Spoken Language Services, Inc., with permission of Otto Harrasowitz, 1994), 776.

7. Qur'an 4:11.

CHAPTER 4

1. Qur'an, Surah al-Baqarah 2:284.

2. *Al-Bukhari*, "Arabic-English Book Reference: Book 59, Hadith, 52, Vol. 4, Book 54, Hadith 464," https://sunnah.com/bukhari/59/52.

3. Jayson Georges, "The Three Kinds of Honor," http://honorshame.com/kinds-of-honor/.

CHAPTER 5

1. Werner Mischke, *The Global Gospel* (Mission ONE, 2015), 23.

CHAPTER 6

1. For an insightful discussion of this subject, see "Ascribed Honor Versus Achieved Honor: What Does it Mean for Cross-Cultural Partnerships?," http://wernermischke.org/2009/11/05/ascribed-honor-versus-achieved-honor-what-does-it-mean-for-cross-cultural-partnerships/.

2. Quran, Surah 3:45, 3:47, 2:136, 19:19, 3:55.

3. Fouad Masri, in *Unlock the Truth: Who Is Isa Bin Maryam* and *Do Christians Worship Three Gods?* (Colorado: Book Villages, 2014), provides a compelling examination of Jesus's identity as Son of God.

CHAPTER 7

1. Muller, Roland, 18.

2. Muller, 41-42.

3. William R. Nicoll, "Commentary on Genesis 3:21," Sermon Bible Commentary, https://www.studylight.org/commentaries/sbc/genesis-3.html.

4. Genesis 38:8; Leviticus 25:25; Deuteronomy 25:5-10.

CHAPTER 8

1. Aduruma tribe (Kenya); Sudan.

2. "Female Genital Mutilation: Key Facts," last modified January 31, 2018, http://www.who.int/news-room/fact-sheets/detail/female-genital-mutilation. According to the World Health Organization's definition, "female genital mutilation (FGM) includes procedures that intentionally alter or cause injury to the female genital organs for non-medical reasons."

3. http://www.who.int/news-room/fact-sheets/detail/female-genital-mutilation.

4. Kathy Gannon, "'I Had To:' Inside the Mind of an Honor Killer in Pakistan," APnews.com, accessed November 9, 2018, https://www.apnews.com/0ddcb44fe2b9416381e44ad35c07314b/%22I-had-to:%22-Inside-the-mind-of-an-'honor'-killer-in-Pakistan.

5. Psalm 107:7; Proverbs 3:6.

CHAPTER 9

1. John R. Kohlenberger III and James Swanson, *A Concise Dictionary of the Greek* (Michigan: Zondervan, 1996), 3666. John 1:14; 18; 3:16, 18; 1 John 4:9.

2. According to the *Amplified Bible* (La Habra, CA: Lockman Foundation, 2015), in footnote to Leviticus 16:8, the term means "goat of removal" or is otherwise a name. This goat's release (16:10) symbolized the carrying away of Israel's sin.

3. M.G. Easton MA, DD, *Illustrated Bible Dictionary*, 3rd ed. https://www.biblestudytools.com/dictionary/azazel/.

4. "Strong's #3371, (Greek) *meketi,*" https://www.bibletools.org/index.cfm/fuseaction/Lexicon. show/ID/G3371/meketi.htm.

5. "Strong's #264, (Greek) hamartano," https://www.bibletools.org/index.cfm/fuseaction/Lexicon. show/ID/G264/hamartano.htm.

6. "The Rules of the Pharisees," pursueGOD.org, accessed November 9, 2018, http://www.pursue god.org/rules-pharisees/.

CHAPTER 10

1. Old Testament Lexical Aid, 3883, found also in Exodus 16:17; 1 Samuel 4:21-22; 2 Chronicles 5:14; Psalm 19:1; 57:5,11; Isaiah 40:5, *Hebrew Greek Key Word Study Bible*, NIV, AMG International, 1996.

2. New Testament Lexical Aid, 1518, *Hebrew Greek Key Word Study Bible*, NIV, AMG International, 1996.

3. Jayson Georges, "The Problem with Bible Translations: Your Culture," http://honorshame.com/ problem-of-culture.

4. For a more extensive discussion of the Muslim beliefs about the death of Jesus, see Fouad Masri's book *Who Died on the Cross?* Indianapolis IN: Crescent Projects n.d.

5. New Testament Lexical Aid, 1518, *Hebrew Greek Key Word Study Bible*, NIV, AMG International, 1996.

6. For an in-depth look at how man can shame God, read the article "Can You Shame God?" at HonorShame.com.

CHAPTER 11

1. John Kohlenberger and James Swanson, *A Concise Dictionary of the Greek* (Grand Rapids, MI: Zondervan, 1996) 4155.

2. Maher Khattab, "Lessons from Hijrah," Muslim Association of Britain, https://www.mabonline .net/about-islam/lessons-from-hijrah/.

3. *Sahih al Bukhari*, Book 15:9, Number 583.

4. Dr. Riffat Hassan, Pakistani-American theologian and Islamic feminist scholar, gives a fascinating exposition and commentary on who she calls her "foremother," Hagar (*Hajira* in Arabic) within the Abrahamic narrative of Islam in "Islamic Hagar and Her Family," *Hagar, Sarah and Their Children*, eds. Phyllis Trible and Letty M. Russel (Westminster Knox Press, 2006), 149-67.

5. Strong's Concordance, 5781a. 'ayin.

6. Wehr, Hans Wehr, *The Hans Wehr Dictionary of Modern Written Arabic*, ed. J. M. Cowan, (Urbana: Spoken Language Services, Inc., 1994), 776, with permission of Otto Harrasowitz, https://www.biblestudytools.com/dictionary/ayin/.

7. In Islam, it is permissible for Muslim men to marry Christian or Jewish women, called in Arabic *kitabiyyah,* "women of the Book" (see Qur'an Al-Ma'idah, 5). Muslim women, however, are not afforded the same right.

8. (Hebrew) *derek,* 1870: going, walk, journey, way, path, manner, way of life, lot in life. (Old Testament Lexical Aid, *Hebrew Greek Key Word Study Bible*, NASB, AMG International, 1996).

9. Study Notes on Genesis 16:11, *Hebrew Greek Key Word Study Bible*, NIV, AMG International, 1996.

10. (Hebrew) *qārā,* 7924. Old Testament Lexical Aid, *Hebrew Greek Key Word Study Bible*, NASB, AMG International, 1996.

11. (Hebrew) *rā'ah,* 8011. Old Testament Lexical Aid, *Hebrew Greek Key Word Study Bible,* NASB, AMG International, 1996.

12. John R. Kohlenberger III and James Swanson, *A Concise Dictionary of the Hebrew* (Grand Rapids, MI: Zondervan Publishing House, 1996), 936.

CHAPTER 12

1. "(Greek) *haptō:* implies a certain degree of involvement with the object on the part of the subject, more than mere contact or touch, but an engagement, handling, or use in which some kind of influence or effect is created between the items coming into contact." *New Testament Lexical Aid,* 721, *Hebrew Greek Key Word Study Bible,* NIV, AMG International, 1996.

2. (Greek) *psēlaphaō,* 6027, New Testament Lexical Aid, 721, *Hebrew Greek Key Word Study Bible,* NIV, AMG International, 1996.

CHAPTER 13

1. "Men are in charge of women by [right of] what Allah has given one over the other and what they spend [for maintenance] from their wealth. So righteous women are devoutly obedient, guarding in [the husband's] absence what Allah would have them guard. But those [wives] from whom you fear arrogance—[first] advise them; [then if they persist], forsake them in bed; and [finally], strike them. But if they obey you [once more], seek no means against them. Indeed, Allah is ever Exalted and Grand" (Qur'an 4:34). The interpretation of this passage is widely debated among contemporary Muslim apologists. Modern Muslims are hesitant to say that Islam promotes domestic violence. However, in many parts of the Muslim world, the practice is widespread and accepted without examination or question.

2. *herem* (Hebrew) 3051: from *haram,* to destroy totally, devote. Something devoted unto divine service; a person or thing marked for destruction. Often used in the sense of something forbidden, prohibited. (Old Testament Lexical Aid, *Hebrew Greek Key Word Study Bible,* NIV, AMG International, 1996).

CHAPTER 14

1. *Salat* is Arabic for obligatory, ritual prayer performed five times per day by Muslims. *Salat-al-maghrib* is the fourth prayer period of the day, occurring just after sunset. *Salat* is the second of the five pillars of Islam. From age seven, Muslim girls and boys are encouraged to pray the five daily prayers of *salat.*

2. *Salat* rules for girls and boys are different. Girls and women must perform ritual prayers with special consideration of concealment, or physical discretion. This principle dictates the covering of all body parts except face, hands, and feet, consequently requiring modified positions during praying such as only lifting the hands to the shoulders (which would risk exposure of the female's wrists or forearms) instead of extending them to the ears as males do.

3. The *qiblah* is Arabic for the direction of the Kaaba, a stone structure in Mecca. The Kaaba is the most sacred site in Islam. Muslims are to face the Kaaba when they perform *salat,* or prayer.

4. Some Islamic schools of thought encourage boys and girls as young as seven to begin their daily prayers.

5. Sahih al-Bukhari, Volume 5, Book 58, Number 234.

6. Qur'an 33:37.

7. Qur'an 4:24.

8. Deuteronomy 2:20; 11:22; 13:4; 30:20; Joshua 23:8; 2 Kings 18:6; Psalm 119:31-32.

9. Study Notes on Ruth, *Hebrew Greek Key Word Study Bible*, NIV, AMG International, 1996.

10. Monica Rey discusses Ruth's ethnical and religious background in her probing master's thesis "Intersectionality in the Book of Ruth: Constructing Ruth's Identity in Ancient Israel," Boston University School of Theology, 2012. Chemosh, god of the Moabites, is discussed extensively in other sources, including Britannica.com, christogea.org, and bible-history.com.

11. Ruth 2:1 (Hebrew) *hayil*, 2657 (Old Testament Lexical Aid, *Hebrew Greek Key Word Study Bible*, NIV, AMG International, 1996).

CHAPTER 15

1. Bill Bright, *The Four Spiritual Laws* (New Life Publications, 1993).

2. *Tabiba* is Arabic for doctor and is often used to describe various other medical workers. In my case, although I was not a doctor, it was the title I was given as a speech-language pathologist. My attempts to clarify my role were met with dismissal, and the name stuck whether I liked it or not. I examined patients, made decisions about their surgery, worked in the operating room, and wore scrubs. I carried children into surgery and delivered them to their mothers afterward. As far as the patients were concerned, I was a *tabiba*.

CHAPTER 16

1. https://www.bible-history.com/backd2/engraving_palms.html.

2. Nadia Murad, *The Last Girl* (New York: Tim Duggan Books, 2017), 115-16.

CHAPTER 17

1. Sayed Naqibullah, "What Does Ghairat Mean in Pashto," February 24, 2013, https://blogs .transparent.com/pashto/what-does-ghairat-mean-in-pashto/.

CHAPTER 18

1. Qur'an, Al Buruj 85:14.

2. Hans Wehr, *The Hans Wehr Dictionary of Modern Written Arabic,* ed. J.M. Cowan, 1241 (Urbana: Spoken Language Services, Inc., 1994), 1241, with permission of Otto Harrasowitz.

3. Wehr, 179.

4. Jinan Yousef, "Love Is in Giving: Al Wadud," http://www.virtualmosque.com/islam-studies/ islam-101/belief-and-worship/love-is-in-giving-al-wadud/.

5. Al-Bukhari, "Arabic-English Book Reference: Book 1, Hadith, 386," https://sunnah.com/riya dus-saliheen/1/386, emphasis added.

HONOR AND SHAME KEY APPLICATIONS

1. Luke 7:37 (Greek) *hamartōlos*, 283, New Testament Lexical Aid, *Hebrew Greek Key Word Study Bible,* NIV, AMG International, 1996.

Additional Resources

BOOKS:

Honor and Shame: Unlocking the Door by Roland Muller (Xlibris, 2001)

The 3D Gospel by Jayson Georges (Tim& 275 Press, 2014)

Ministering in Honor-Shame Cultures by Jayson Georges and Mark D. Baker (IVP, 2016)

The Global Gospel by Werner Mischke (Mission One, 2014)

Shame and Honor in the Book of Esther by Timothy Laniak (Society of Biblical Literature, 1998)

Honor, Patronage, Kinship, and Purity by David deSilva (IVP Academic, 2000)

Restoring the Shamed by Robin Stockitt (Wipf & Stock Publishers, 2012)

WEBSITES:

HonorShame.com

jacksonwu.org

RealHonour.com

www.audreyfrank.com

whenwomenspeak.net

Audrey Frank is an author, speaker, and storyteller. The stories she shares are brave and true. They give voice to those whose words are silenced by shame, the hard things in life that don't make sense, and the losses that leave us wondering if we will survive.

Audrey and her family have spent over 20 years living and working among Muslim cultures and various worldviews, and she has found that God's story of redemption spans every geography and culture. He is the God of *Instead*, giving honor *instead* of shame, gladness *instead* of mourning, hope *instead* of despair. Audrey holds a BS in communication disorders, an MA in speech-language pathology, and a BA in biblical and intercultural studies. However, her greatest credential is that she is known and loved by the One who made her.

You can also find Audrey at www.audreyfrank.com, as well as on Twitter (@audreycfrank) and Facebook.